Windows® 10 For Seniors

4th Edition

by Peter Weverka

for dummies®
A Wiley Brand

Windows® 10 For Seniors For Dummies®, 4th Edition

Published by: **John Wiley & Sons, Inc.**, 111 River Street, Hoboken, NJ 07030-5774, www.wiley.com

Copyright © 2020 by John Wiley & Sons, Inc., Hoboken, New Jersey

Published simultaneously in Canada

For general information on our other products and services, please contact our Customer Care Department within the U.S. at 877-762-2974, outside the U.S. at 317-572-3993, or fax 317-572-4002. For technical support, please visit https://hub.wiley.com/community/support/dummies.

Wiley publishes in a variety of print and electronic formats and by print-on-demand. Some material included with standard print versions of this book may not be included in e-books or in print-on-demand. If this book refers to media such as a CD or DVD that is not included in the version you purchased, you may download this material at http://booksupport.wiley.com. For more information about Wiley products, visit www.wiley.com.

Library of Congress Control Number: 2020935782

ISBN: 978-1-119-68054-3

ISBN 978-1-119-68056-7 (ebk); ISBN ePDF 978-1-119-68053-6 (ebk)

Manufactured in the United States of America

SKY10020001_072220

Contents at a Glance

Table of Contents

Introduction

Windows 10, April 2020 release, is the latest generation of Microsoft's operating system, the master program that makes a computer useful and provides support to other programs, including word processors, photo viewers, and web browsers. Much as an education equips you to read a novel or play a game, Windows 10 equips your computer to perform a wide range of activities. You can use Windows 10 and other software (or *apps*) to read or write a novel, play games or music, and stay in touch with friends and family around the world.

As Windows has evolved over the past 30 years, so have computers — the *hardware.* Today, you can buy a computer as small as a paperback book, and even such a little computer is unimaginably more powerful than (and a fraction of the cost of) computers just 10 years ago. The hardware consists of the screen, as well as optional components such as a keyboard and a mouse.

You don't need much time with a computer to conclude that there has to be an easier way to do things. At times, computers seem overly complex and inscrutable. Have you used a cellphone lately? Or a TV remote control? Why are the controls on every microwave oven different? Why does every new tool offer countless options you don't want that obscure the ones you do want? Well, I don't have the answers to those questions, but I do have step-by-step instructions for many tasks you want to perform using Windows 10.

After many years of working with computers, I find that they reward patience, curiosity, and a little methodical exploration. Seniors, in particular, know that learning never really stops and that learning new things keeps one young, at least figuratively. By the end of this book, you may be a multitasking computerist performing virtual gymnastics with Windows 10. On the other hand, if this book helps you do only one thing — use email, browse the web, or enjoy photos or music — that one useful thing may be all you need.

About This Book

Age is just a number. This book is intended for anyone getting started with Windows 10 who wants step-by-step instructions without a lot of discussion. Numerous figures with notes show you the computer screen as you progress through the steps. Reading this book is like having an experienced friend stand behind you as you use Windows 10 . . . someone who never takes control of the computer away from you.

Windows 10 is a work in progress. Microsoft updates the Windows 10 operating system from time to time to make it more secure and agreeable to the people who use it. (Chapter 3 explains how to check for updates to Windows 10.) Because the operating system is continuously updated, the screen shots you see in this book may not exactly match what you see on your screen.

Conventions Used in This Book

This book uses certain conventions to highlight important information and help you find your way around:

» Different **methods for performing steps:** In general, you can complete a step in three ways. I list the choices as follows:

- **Mouse:** If you have a mouse, follow these instructions.
- **Touchscreen:** You may be able to touch your screen to perform tasks.
- **Keyboard:** Keyboard shortcuts are often the fastest way to do something.

When you have a choice between these methods, experiment to determine which is easiest for you.

» **Tip icons:** Point out helpful suggestions related to tasks in the step lists.

TIP

» **Bold:** I use bold for figure references as well as for when you have to type something onscreen using the keyboard.

Many figures have notes or other markings to draw your attention to a specific part of the figure. The text tells you what to look for; the figure notes help you find it.

» **Website addresses:** If you bought an e-book, website addresses are live links. In the text, website addresses look like this: www.dummies.com. See Chapter 6 for information on browsing the web.

» **Options and buttons:** Although Windows 10 often uses lower-case in options and on buttons, I capitalize the text for emphasis. That way, you can find a button labeled Save Now, even though onscreen it appears as *Save now*.

How to Read This Book

You can work through this book from beginning to end or simply look at the table of contents or index to find the instructions you need to solve a problem or learn a new skill whenever you need it. The steps in each task get you where you want to go quickly, without a lot of technical explanation. In no time, you'll start picking up the skills you need to become a confident Windows 10 user.

Technology always comes with its own terms and concepts, but you don't need to learn another language to use a computer. You don't need any prior experience with computers or Windows. Step-by-step instructions guide you through specific tasks, such as accessing the news or playing a game. These steps provide just the information you need for the task at hand.

Foolish Assumptions

I assume that you have a computer and want clear, brief, step-by-step instructions on getting things done with Windows 10. I assume also that you want to know just what you need to know, just when you need to know it. This isn't Computers 101. This is Practical Windows 10. As an old friend of mine said, "I don't want to make a watch; I just want to know what time it is."

How This Book Is Organized

This book is divided into four parts to help you find what you need. You can read from cover to cover or just jump to the page that interests you.

» **Part 1: Getting Started with Windows 10:** In Chapter 1, you turn on the computer and get comfortable with essential parts of Windows 10, such as the Start screen, as well as how to use a mouse, touchscreen, or keyboard. Explore features of Windows 10 apps in Chapter 2. To customize Windows 10 to work better for you, turn to Chapter 3. In Chapter 4, you create and modify user account settings, such as passwords. Discover the desktop, how to manage windows, and how to customize the desktop in Chapter 5.

» **Part 2: Windows 10 and the Web:** Use the web to stay current and keep in touch. Turn to Chapter 6 to use Edge to browse the web. Send and receive email in Chapter 7. Turn to Chapter 8 to explore a handful of apps that can help you stay in touch with friends and get to know the outside world better.

» **Part 3: Having Fun with Windows 10:** If you haven't been having any fun until now, I've failed you. Expand your tools and toys in Chapter 9 by connecting to Microsoft Store to install new apps. In Chapter 10, you enjoy photos on Windows 10 and put your own photos on the computer. If you want to listen to music and watch a video, see Chapter 11.

» **Part 4: Beyond the Basics:** In Chapter 12, you learn about the care and feeding of Windows 10, which requires a little maintenance now and then. Find out how to connect a printer and other hardware, such as a mouse and a second screen, in Chapter 13. Do you appreciate the saying "a place for everything and everything in its place"? Chapter 14 is where you organize your documents. And finally, you back up your files to insure against loss and refresh Windows 10 when it gets cranky, in Chapter 15.

Beyond the Book

In addition to what you're reading right now, this book comes with a free, access-anywhere Cheat Sheet that helps you minimize all windows but the one you're actively using, schedule an event without opening the Calendar app, view file extensions in File Explorer, and take a screenshot. To get this Cheat Sheet, simply go to www.dummies.com and search for "Windows 10 For Seniors For Dummies Cheat Sheet" by using the Search box.

1

Getting Started with Windows 10

Chapter **1**

Getting Acquainted with Windows 10

Windows 10 is an *operating system* (the master program for any computer). You can use Windows 10 on a wide range of devices, from a smartphone to a big-screen TV/ entertainment system: One size fits most. You can not only use the same programs with a range of hardware but also access the documents you create (such as photos and email — files and data, to nerds) from any Windows-based computer, giving you extraordinary freedom of choice and mobility.

Although countless companies create programs you may use, Microsoft attempts to make similar functions consistent across different programs. For example, opening a document or emailing a photo to a friend involves the same steps regardless of the programs you use. You don't have to learn a different way of doing common tasks in each program. This consistency will serve you well when using Windows 10 and other new programs.

In this chapter, you start your computer and work with the *Start screen*, the dashboard for Windows 10. You explore options for using the Start screen with your *hardware* (the computer and related devices). Then you exit Windows 10 and go right back in for more.

The easiest way to get Windows 10 is preinstalled on a new computer. If your current computer runs an older version of (Windows 7, Windows 8, or Windows 8.1), you can upgrade to Windows 10, although older machines may lack newer functions, such as a touchscreen.

Tell Your Computer What to Do

How do you get Windows 10 to do what you want it to do? You can command a computer in many ways, depending on your equipment (hardware). For example, a desktop computer has different options from a handheld phone. You may have any or all of these choices:

» Mouse

» Touchscreen

» Keyboard

Another device for controlling Windows is a touchpad, which is commonly found on a laptop keyboard. You move your finger on the touchpad to move the pointer on the screen.

If you have a computer with more than one of these devices, you might use one device exclusively or, more likely, vary your choice according to the task. Use whichever technique is easiest for you, but don't be afraid to experiment. In the next few sections, you discover the ins and outs of using all these methods of controlling Windows 10. Then you're ready to turn on your computer and use these methods.

In the steps throughout this book, *choose* or *select* refers to using a mouse, the touchscreen, or a physical keyboard. *Drag* refers to using a mouse or a finger.

Move the Mouse

A *mouse* is a soap–bar–sized device that you move across a desk with your hand. Move the mouse and note how the arrow called a *mouse pointer* moves across the computer screen. (Similar to a mouse, a *trackball* is a ball in a socket that you can rotate to move the mouse pointer.) A mouse has two or more buttons; some also have a scroll wheel between the buttons.

The following terms describe methods for using a mouse with Windows 10. In each, move the mouse first to position the pointer over a specified item before proceeding:

» **Click:** Move the onscreen arrow-shaped mouse pointer over a specified item and press and release the left mouse button: That's a click (sometimes called a left-click to distinguish it from a right-click).

» **Right-click:** Press and release the right mouse button to display available functions. Note that the word *click* by itself means use the left mouse button.

» **Drag:** Press and hold down the left mouse button, and then move the mouse pointer across the screen. When you want to move an object, you drag it. Release the mouse button to release the object.

Watch for the word *click* to indicate using a mouse button and *roll* to indicate using the mouse wheel.

TIP

Touch the Screen

A *touchscreen*, as the name says, enables you to touch the screen to tell your computer what to do. You typically use one finger or two, although touchscreens may allow you to use all ten digits. In some cases, you can also use a special pen called a *stylus* instead of your finger. Tablet computers and some smartphones have touchscreens. Touchscreens are less common on desktop or laptop computers, but that situation is changing. Not sure what type of screen you have? When you have Windows 10 running, give the screen a gentle poke with your index finger to see what happens.

The following terms refer to ways you interact with a touchscreen:

» **Tap:** Briefly touch the screen. You *select* an object, such as a button, by tapping it.

» **Drag:** Touch and hold your finger on the screen, then move your finger across the screen. You *move* an object, such as an onscreen playing card, by dragging it.

» **Swipe:** Touch and move your finger more quickly than with drag. You can swipe your finger across the screen from any of the four sides of the screen to display options and commands. You swipe pages to move forward or back. You may see the word *flick* instead of *swipe.* Some people insist that a flick is faster or shorter than a swipe, but let's not get caught up in that.

» **Pinch and unpinch:** Touch a finger and thumb or two fingers on the screen. Move your fingers closer to each other to *pinch* and away from each other to *unpinch.* Generally, a pinch reduces the size of something on the screen or shows more content on the screen. An unpinch (an ugly word) *zooms in,* increasing the size of something onscreen to show more detail.

Watch for the words *tap, swipe,* or *pinch* to indicate using your finger. Touch actions are often called *gestures.*

See the upcoming section "View the Touch Keyboard" if your computer doesn't have a physical keyboard, as is often the case with a touchscreen.

Use a Keyboard

A typewriter-like keyboard is a traditional device for controlling a computer and is especially useful when you must enter a lot of text. Special key combinations, called *shortcut keys*, are often the quickest way to do anything (though they require some memorization).

The following keys are particularly noteworthy. No offense intended to fans of keys not noted here. Although you won't use all these keys immediately, you'll find it helpful to locate each one on your keyboard.

TIP

Press indicates that you use the keyboard (physical or virtual) for the specified key or sequence of keys (just as *click* indicates a mouse action and *tap* indicates touch). Combinations of keys are not pressed simultaneously. Instead, press and hold the first key in the specified sequence, press the second key, and then release both. (I explain exceptions to this method as necessary.)

» ⊞: Called the Windows key, this key is usually located on either side of the spacebar, which is the largest key. ⊞ works by itself, as you'll soon see, and also in combination with many other keys. Throughout the book, I specify these combinations where you might use them. There will be a quiz later. (Kidding! No quizzes.)

» **Tab:** Press the Tab key to highlight an item. Press Tab repeatedly to skip items you don't intend to select.

TIP

The keyboard can be used to select objects but is less direct than using touch or a mouse.

» **Arrow keys:** Press the arrow keys to move the cursor or selection of an object in the direction the keys point (left, right, up, or down). In some contexts, Tab and the right arrow do the same thing. Sorry to be vague, but context matters at times.

» **Enter:** In most cases, the Enter key on the keyboard chooses a selection, much as clicking or tapping does. However, you may need to use the Tab key or an arrow key to select an item before pressing the Enter key.

» **Ctrl, Alt,** and **Shift keys:** These keys are used with other keys for commands. For example, press Ctrl+C to copy selected text or an object. (That is, while pressing and holding down the Ctrl key, press the C key — no need to press Shift for an uppercase C. Then release both keys.) The Shift key is used with another key for uppercase.

» **Backspace:** As you enter text, each press of Backspace erases the character to the left of the cursor.

» **Delete:** As you enter text, each press of the Delete key erases the character to the right of the cursor. On some keyboards, this key is labeled Del.

» **Function keys:** All keys function, but Function keys are labeled F1 through F12. You don't use these much in this book, but you should locate them. Laptops often have a separate Function Lock key to turn these keys on or off.

» **Page keys:** Locate the Home, End, Page Up, and Page Down keys for future reference. Use these to move the screen, a page, or the cursor. (On some keyboards, the Home, End, Page Up, and Page Down keys work as numbers when the Num Lock key is activated.)

View the Touch Keyboard

Windows 10 can display a touch keyboard onscreen. This feature is vital for devices that have a touchscreen and no physical keyboard. With a touchscreen, the touch keyboard appears automatically when the *cursor* (a blinking vertical bar) indicates that you can enter text in a box. If the touch keyboard doesn't appear automatically, you may also see a separate box floating above or below the text box. Tap that floating box to display the keyboard. To type using the keyboard, simply tap or click a letter, number, or symbol key.

TIP

Here are the different types of touch keyboards:

» The *standard layout* (also called QWERTY) appears automatically (see **Figure 1-1**). The Enter key changes depending on the context.

» The *uppercase layout,* shown in **Figure 1-2,** appears when you tap the Shift key on the standard layout.

» The *numbers and symbols layout,* shown in **Figure 1-3,** appears when you tap the &123 key on the standard layout. Tap the &123 key again to return to the standard layout.

» The control keys overlay (see **Figure 1-4**) appears on five keys on the standard layout when you tap the Ctrl key. The Ctrl keys are used in common tasks, such as copying (Ctrl+C) or moving (Ctrl+X) selected text. The overlay disappears automatically after you tap one of the control keys (A, Z, X, C, or V).

» The *emoji layout,* shown in **Figure 1-5,** appears when you tap the Smiley Face key. Tap the Smiley Face key again to return to the standard layout. (Emojis are also called *emoticons* or *smileys.*)

Tap (or press Esc) to close the touch keyboard

FIGURE 1-1

FIGURE 1-2

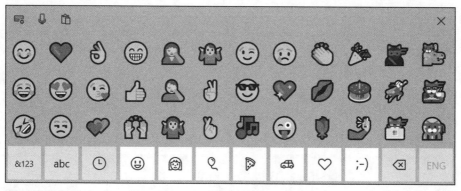

FIGURE 1-3

FIGURE 1-4

FIGURE 1-5

TIP

To quickly enter an emoji without opening the touch keyboard, press ⊞+period (.). The emoji panel appears. Click or tap an emoji to enter it onscreen.

But wait! There's more. Tap the keyboard key, which is in the upper-left corner of any layout, to display the five options shown in **Figure 1-6.**

» Tap the Standard button (refer to **Figure 1-6**) to return to the standard layout from one of the other layouts.

» Tap the Narrow button to see a narrow keyboard suitable for thumb typing.

» Tap the Split button to view the *split keyboard layout,* shown in **Figure 1-7.** This layout is handy for typing with your thumbs while holding two sides of a tablet.

» Tap the Expanded button to view a keyboard with keys such as Tab, Caps Lock, and Shift that appear on a conventional keyboard.

» Tap the Handwriting button to view the *handwriting layout,* shown in **Figure 1-8.** This layout enables you to write with a finger or a stylus (a special pen). Windows converts your scribbles to block text (if it can make sense of your scribbles).

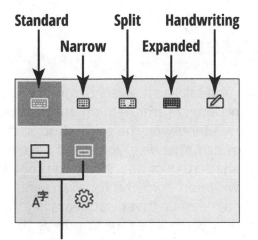

Widen or narrow the keyboard

FIGURE 1-6

FIGURE 1-7

FIGURE 1-8

The keyboard pop-up menu also offers buttons for widening or narrowing the keyboard on the bottom of the screen (refer to **Figure 1-6**).

TIP

Turn On Your Computer

1. Push the power button briefly and release it. Every computer has a power button. (When we can no longer turn them off, the machines win.) If you have a desktop computer tower, the power button is probably on the front of the tower. Otherwise, you might have to feel around the front and sides of the screen or near the hinges of a laptop. Typically, your computer will beep, some buttons will light, and the screen may flash a logo or a message that disappears before you can read it. (Just let that go.) Soon, you will see the Windows 10 Lock screen.

2. Turn on any separate hardware (such as a monitor, speakers, or a printer), if necessary.

3. Enter your password and press Enter (or select the Submit button, the button on the right side of the password textbox). Soon the Windows 10 desktop screen appears, as shown in **Figure 1-9.**

FIGURE 1-9

TIP

If you don't see the Password text box, jiggle the mouse or press a key on the keyboard to wake up Windows 10.

The first time you turn on a new computer, a series of Windows Setup screens appears. Accept the defaults or change them appropriately and then select the button labeled Next.

If your computer doesn't have a keyboard, as is the case with many tablet computers, see the preceding section, "View the Touch Keyboard," for information on how to type onscreen.

If this is the first time that Windows 10 has started on your computer, you must create a user account, even if no one else will use the machine. See Chapter 4 for details on creating and changing user accounts.

Check Out the Start Screen

1. Start your computer — if it isn't started already — and sign in to your user account. You'll see the Windows desktop screen (refer to **Figure 1-9**).

2. Open the Start screen, as shown in **Figure 1-10.** Use one of these methods to open the Start screen:

- **Mouse:** Click the Start button (you'll find it in the lower-left corner of the screen).

- **Touchscreen:** Tap the Start button.

- **Keyboard:** Press the ⊞ key.

FIGURE 1-10

3. Examine the Start screen and note the colorful rectangular icons called *tiles.* These tiles represent available *apps* (short for application programs, an older term for programs or software). By clicking or tapping an app tile, you can open an app. After you start to use the app tiles, they may display changing information, such as the current weather. (See Chapter 2 for information on using individual apps.)

4. Scroll down the names of apps on the left side of the Start screen. You see an alphabetical list of all the apps that are installed on your computer, as shown in **Figure 1-11, left.** By clicking or tapping an app in this list, you can open an app. Scroll on the Start screen when you want to open an application but can't find its tile.

TIP

Under "Most Used," the Start screen lists apps you recently opened. You can click or tap an app name on the Most Used list to open an app.

TIP

While the Start screen is open, you can type the name of an app to open it. For example, to open the Weather app, type **weather.** A panel opens with the names of apps that include the word *weather* (you also see apps from the Microsoft Store and web pages with the word *weather*). Select the Weather app listing in the panel to open the Weather app.

5. Scroll through the alphabetical apps list to Windows Administrative Tools, and then click or tap the down-arrow to the right of the name *Windows Administrative Tools*. As shown in **Figure 1-11, middle,** a list of apps appears under the Windows Administrative Tools heading.

FIGURE 1-11

TIP

In the alphabetical apps list, some names are really headings, not apps. The down arrows tell you where the headings are. Click or tap a down arrow to see the list of apps under a heading.

TIP

Rather than scroll through the alphabetical list to find an app, you can select a letter in the list and then select a letter in the pop-up list of letters that appears (refer to **Figure 1-11, right**). For example, to quickly get to the Weather app, select any letter and then select the W on the pop-up list.

6. Notice the buttons in the lower-left corner of the Start screen. From top to bottom, these buttons are your image, Documents, Pictures, Settings, and Power, as shown in **Figure 1-12.**

TIP

Rather than buttons, you can see button names on the Start screen (see **Figure 1-12**) by selecting the menu button in the upper-left corner of the Start screen.

FIGURE 1-12

7. Click or tap your image (or image and name) on the Start screen. As shown in **Figure 1-13,** you see a pop-up menu with commands for changing account settings (see Chapter 3), locking your screen (see "Start Again on the Lock Screen," later in this chapter), and signing out in a favor of another person who shares your computer (see Chapter 4). Who would think that clicking your name would open a pop-up menu?

- **Touchscreen:** Tap the Start button.
- **Keyboard:** Press the ⊞ key.

2. Click or tap Power on the Start menu (refer to **Figure 1-14**).

3. Available options appear in a pop-up box. Some or all of the following options appear:

- **Sleep:** This option reduces the computer's power consumption without exiting Windows 10 or closing apps (some computers don't offer this option). As a result, when you wake the computer by moving the mouse or touching the screen or the keyboard, everything is exactly as you left it: Apps and documents are open, if they were open before Sleep.

- **Shut Down:** This option exits Windows 10 and saves power by turning the computer off. In exiting Windows 10, Shut Down closes any apps that are currently running.

- **Hibernate:** This option combines Sleep and Shut Down. Hibernate records which apps are running but also completely shuts down the computer. When you start the computer, Windows 10 opens all programs you were using, just as Sleep does.

Hibernate and Shut Down are equally green options — they save the same amount of power. Sleep is a little less green but saves time if you are returning to the middle of a task.

- **Restart:** Temporarily shuts down Windows 10 and turns it on again. Use Restart when Windows 10 asks you to or when Windows 10 is misbehaving.

You can also shut down your computer by using the Start button. Move the pointer over the Start button and right-click. A pop-up menu appears. Select Shut Down or Sign Out on the pop-up menu, and then select an option (Sleep, Shut Down, Hibernate, or Restart).

4. Choose Shut Down to turn off the computer.

On most computers, pressing the power switch also shuts down the computer. On a laptop, closing the lid may shut down the laptop or put it in sleep or hibernation mode.

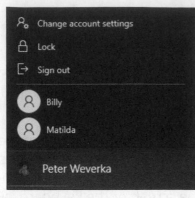

FIGURE 1-13

8. Click or tap Power on the Start menu. As shown in **Figure 1-14,** you see a pop-up menu with commands for putting your computer to sleep, shutting down your computer, and restarting your computer. Later in this chapter, "Shut Down Your Computer" looks into the options on this pop-up menu.

9. Click or tap the Start button, or press the ■ key. Doing any of these actions when the Start screen is open closes the Start screen. You can also close the Start screen by clicking anywhere on the desktop when the Start screen is open.

FIGURE 1-14

Shut Down Your Computer

1. When you have finished using your computer for a while, you may want to shut down Windows 10. Begin by displaying the Start screen:

   - **Mouse:** Click the Start button (located in the lower-left corner of the screen).

TIP

For a desktop computer, consider using a power strip to plug in the computer, the monitor, and the printer. After you shut down or hibernate the computer, turn off the power strip to save power.

Start Again on the Lock Screen

1. Turn on your computer. Every time you turn on your computer, the Lock screen appears. As shown in **Figure 1-15,** the Lock screen displays the time, day, and date along with a photo. (You discover how to change this photo in Chapter 3.)

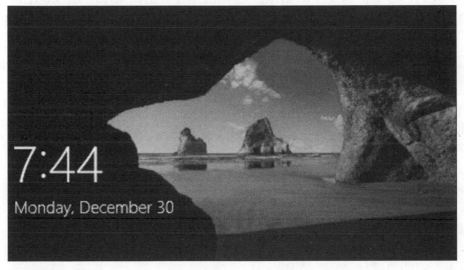

7:44

Monday, December 30

FIGURE 1-15

2. Dismiss the Lock screen with one of these methods:

- **Mouse:** Click anywhere, roll the wheel toward you, or drag the entire screen up.

- **Touchscreen:** Drag the entire screen up.

- **Keyboard:** Press any key.

3. If you don't use a password, wait briefly for the Start screen to appear. If you use a password, enter it with a physical or touch keyboard. Then press Enter or select the arrow next to the password box to display the Windows desktop screen.

4. Take a break before reading Chapter 2.

TIP

When you take a long break from your PC, it automatically goes to sleep. Windows 10 puts your computer to sleep to save battery life. To decide for yourself how much time passes before your computer goes to sleep, select the Settings button and choose Personalization on the Windows Settings screen. Then, on the Personalization screen, choose Lock Screen. Scroll down the screen to the Screen Timeout Settings link and select this link. You come to the Power & Sleep screen. Choose a setting from the Sleep menu. For example, choose 15 minutes to put your computer to sleep after 15 minutes of inactivity.

IN THIS CHAPTER

» Opening, closing, and switching
between apps

» Introducing the app bar

» Tweaking app settings

» Rearranging app tiles on the
Start screen

Chapter **2**

Using the Start Screen and Apps

The Windows 10 *Start screen* appears when you select the Start button in the lower-left corner of the screen or you press the ⊞ key. It provides access to just about everything you do with Windows 10.

The Start screen is home to numerous programs, or *apps* (short for applications). An app performs a function or displays information. For example, the Weather app offers weather reports (surprise!) and the Maps app helps you map a route between two places. Apps can be simple or complex.

Apps appear on the Start screen as *tiles.* A tile, which may be square or rectangular, displays the app's name and symbol or icon. A tile that displays changing information is called a *live tile.* An open app typically covers the screen, hiding other apps that are open. However, some apps can be displayed side-by-side with a function called *snap.*

Two categories of apps are available:

» *Windows 10 apps* are modern looking and rich with information. They are designed to work with touchscreens as well as with a mouse. Weather and Edge are the first two such apps you use in this chapter. (The Maps and Calendar apps function similarly to the Weather app, each with a unique focus.)

» *Desktop apps* always open with the desktop behind them. Most desktop apps don't have the look or consistent functions of Windows 10 apps. Desktop apps may not respond to touch as reliably as Windows 10 apps.

You select an app to use in one of two ways:

» **Mouse:** Move the mouse pointer over an app tile. Click the left mouse button to select the tile and open the app.

» **Touchscreen:** Tap the app tile with one of your fingers.

In this chapter, you open, close, and use some of the apps that come with Windows 10. You also switch between apps and the Start screen, and switch directly between two apps. You find out how to search for apps not shown on the Start screen. Finally, you discover how to organize the Start screen by rearranging tiles into groups.

See Chapter 9 for information on getting new apps from the Micro-soft Store.

Although some steps are specific to one app, most of the steps you follow in this chapter can be repeated in any app.

TIP

Open Windows 10 Apps

1. Select the Start button, as shown in **Figure 2-1.** Selecting this button opens the Start screen, also shown in **Figure 2-1.**

You can also open the Start screen by pressing the ⊞ key.

Weather tile

FIGURE 2-1

2. Use the mouse or a finger to select the Weather tile. (If you've used Weather before, the tile shows a temperature reading in a certain location.) The Weather app opens to the Forecast screen, as shown in **Figure 2-2.** It shows the current temperature and weather forecast for your default location. Select the Show Options button (see **Figure 2-2**). As do most apps, Weather has a Show Options button in the upper-left corner. Select this button to expand the app bar and see the names of options on the app bar. Select the button again to collapse options on the app bar.

TIP

The first time you open the Weather app, a Welcome screen appears. It asks whether you want to show temperatures in Fahrenheit or Celsius and what your location is. By location, the Weather app wants to know where you live, or, if you're a vagabond, where you spend the majority of your time. Choose Detect My Location or enter a city or town name in the Search box, and from the menu that appears as you type, select the name of the town or city that you call home. You can always change these settings by selecting the Settings button in the app bar and choosing options on the Settings screen. (See "Change App Settings," later in this chapter.)

Show Options button

FIGURE 2-2

3. Switch back to the Start screen using one of these methods:

   - Tap or click the Start button.

   - Press the ⊞ key.

   Focus on the method you think is easiest. However, keep in mind that alternative methods of controlling your computer are always available.

4. On the Start screen, check to see whether the Weather tile displays current weather information, as in **Figure 2-3.** The Weather app has a *live tile,* meaning that its tile on the Start screen displays changing information.

5. Switch back to the Weather app by selecting its tile with the mouse or your finger. The Weather app reappears.

6. Switch back to the Start screen.

Weather has a live tile

FIGURE 2-3

7. Select the Microsoft Edge tile (look for a blue icon). The Edge screen appears, as shown in **Figure 2-4.**

TIP

If the Edge tile doesn't appear on your Start screen, scroll in the alphabetical list of apps to the Edge app tile and select it.

Edge is a browser, which is an Internet application for exploring the web. Chapter 6 covers Edge in detail.

TIP

8. Scroll downward to see all that is on the web page you are visiting. Use these techniques to scroll:

- **Mouse:** Drag the scroll box on the right side of the screen up or down. If your mouse has a wheel, you can also turn the mouse wheel to scroll.

- **Touchscreen:** Swipe the screen up or down.

9. Switch to the Start screen by selecting the Windows button or pressing the ■ key.

10. On the Start screen, select the Weather tile. Switch back and forth between the Weather app and the Start screen a few times to get comfortable with switching between an app and the Start screen.

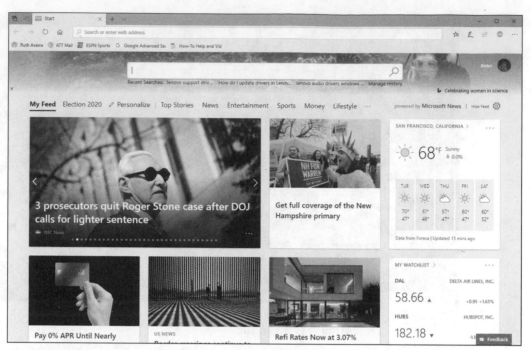

FIGURE 2-4

Switch among Open Apps

1. Open the Weather app, as in the preceding section.

2. Switch to the Start screen and open the Edge app.

3. Switch to Task view, as shown in **Figure 2-5.** In Task view, thumbnail versions of all open apps appear on the screen. You can switch to Task view with one of these methods:

- **Mouse:** Click the Task View button on the taskbar (refer to **Figure 2-5**).

- **Touchscreen:** Swipe from the left edge of the screen or tap the Task View button.

- **Keyboard:** Press ⊞+Tab.

4. Select the Weather app to switch to it. Task view offers one way of switching between apps. Use the Task View method to switch between apps when many apps are open onscreen. Seeing tiles for all open apps makes switching from one app to another easy.

Select a thumbnail to switch apps

Drag to open apps and files you opened in the past

Task View button   **Select an icon to switch apps**

FIGURE 2-5

TIP

Besides offering thumbnail versions of open apps in Task View, Windows 10 also gives you the opportunity to backtrack and open apps you used in days past. Scroll down the screen or drag the slider to see thumbnail pictures of your past activities. Selecting a thumbnail picture opens the app you were using in the past.

TIP

Chapter 5 explains how you can open a second desktop on the screen and in so doing keep some of your open apps on one screen and some of your open apps on another. When you're running many apps, opening a second desktop is a great way to be able to switch quickly from one app to another.

5. Select the Edge app icon on the taskbar to switch to the Edge app (refer to **Figure 2-5**). The taskbar is located along the bottom of the screen. Whenever you open an app, Windows 10 places that app's icon on the taskbar. You can select an icon on the taskbar to switch to an open app.

TIP

Some icons appear permanently on the taskbar. For example, the File Explorer icon is always on the taskbar regardless of whether File Explorer is running. Chapter 5 explains how you can pin your favorite apps to the taskbar. Pinning an app to the taskbar places an icon there so that you can open an app quickly.

6. Press Alt+Tab and continue to hold down the Alt key after you press Tab. A window showing thumbnails of all open apps appears onscreen, as shown in **Figure 2-6**. While holding down the Alt key, press the left- or right-arrow key to select the Weather thumbnail, and then release the Alt key. The Weather app appears onscreen. Pressing Alt+Tab is yet another way to switch between open applications.

FIGURE 2-6

TIP

Chapter 5 demonstrates techniques for moving windows onscreen, changing the size of windows, and snapping windows to the side of the screen.

Close Windows 10 Apps

1. On the Start screen, select the Weather app if the Weather app isn't already open.

2. Close the Weather app (or any open app) with one of these methods:

- **Mouse:** Click the Close button (the X) in the upper-right corner of the screen.

- **Touchscreen:** Tap the Close button (the X) in the upper-right corner of the screen.

- **Keyboard:** Press Alt+F4.

You don't have to close apps. However, having unneeded apps open makes switching between apps more of a challenge because of unneeded thumbnails in the app switcher.

3. On the Start screen again, select the Weather app tile to reopen the Weather app. Notice the Weather app icon on the taskbar along the bottom of the screen.

4. Display the context menu on the Weather app icon and choose Close Window on the context menu, as shown in **Figure 2-7.** Use one of these techniques to display the context menu on a taskbar icon:

- **Mouse:** Right-click the icon.

- **Touchscreen:** Touch and hold the icon until a rectangle appears around the icon, and then release your finger.

You can close an app from the taskbar

FIGURE 2-7

To close an app that is frozen (an app that is unresponsive), press Ctrl+Shift+Esc. The Task Manager opens. It lists all apps that are currently running. Select the app you want to close and then select the End Task button.

Use the App Bar

1. From the Start screen, open the Weather app if it isn't already open.

2. The *app bar* contains functions specific to the current app. Display the app bar by selecting the Show Options button. **Figure 2-8** shows the app bar in the Weather app.

The app bar may appear across the top of the screen, the left side of the screen, or in both locations.

TIP

Show Options button

App bar

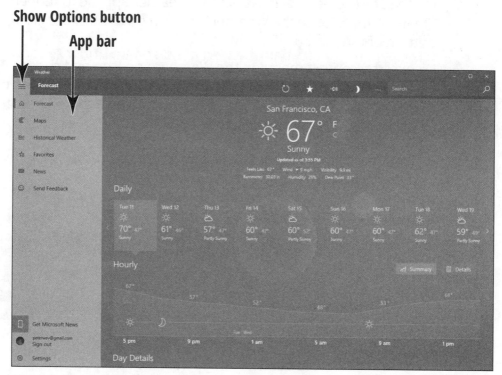

FIGURE 2-8

3. In the Weather app, the app bar leads you to different functions. Select Maps, for example, to see a weather map of the area where you live.

4. Display the app bar in Weather again. Then select News. A screen appears with news stories about weather in the country where you live.

5. Display the app bar again and take notice of the Home icon. Wherever you travel in an app, you can return to the app *home screen* by selecting this icon.

TIP

In most apps, you can select the Back button (a left-pointing arrow) to return to the previous screen you viewed. The Back button is found in the upper-left corner of most screens.

Add a Location in Weather

1. From the Start screen, open the Weather app if it isn't already open. With the Weather app on the screen, select the Show Options button to expand the app bar and see the option names (refer to **Figure 2-8**).

2. Select the Favorites button on the app bar. The Favorites screen appears, as shown in **Figure 2-9.** Your screen will show a different live tile.

FIGURE 2-9

3. Select the Add to Favorites tile, which looks like a plus sign in a square. The Add to Favorites screen appears.

4. Type a location name, such as a city, in the box under Add to Favorites, as shown in **Figure 2-10.** As you type, matching location names appear below the box. If you see the location you want, select that name to add a tile for that location to the Places screen. No need to click the Add button, unless your location does not appear automatically.

TIP

You can add other locations by repeating Steps 3 and 4.

Type in the box

FIGURE 2-10

5. Select the tile for the location you added. The Weather app displays full information for the location you selected.

You can switch among multiple locations by using the Favorites button on the app bar.

6. Return to the Start screen. Your new favorite location does not appear on the Weather tile — yet. Select the Weather tile on the taskbar to return to the Weather app. Notice that, in addition to the app bar on the left side of the screen, an app bar for the selected location appears along the top of the screen.

7. Select the Pin button on the app bar at the top of the screen, as shown in **Figure 2-11.** On the confirmation message box, select Yes. Selecting the Pin button adds a tile for the current location to the Start screen. (If you don't see the Pin button, repeat Steps 2–5 to add a favorite location.)

Pin this location to the Weather app tile on the Start screen

FIGURE 2-11

8. Return to the Start screen. The original Weather tile appears, as well as the new tile. You may have to scroll downward to see the new Weather tile.

9. Select the new Weather tile to open the app with that location.

10. Display the app bar for Weather, which is shown in **Figure 2-12.** Select the Unpin button at the top of the screen to remove the tile for the current location from the Start screen. If the Unpin button doesn't appear, repeat Step 7.

Return to the Start screen. The location you unpinned no longer appears.

Select Unpin

FIGURE 2-12

> **TIP**
>
> Select Favorites in the App bar to see a screen with weather locations you chose (refer to **Figure 2-9**). From there, you can select a weather location to get reports and predictions about weather in a different city or place.

> **TIP**
>
> Add locations for friends, family, and travel destinations and pin these new locations to the Start screen. See "Arrange and Group Apps on the Start Screen," later in this chapter, if you want to group these tiles.

Change App Settings

1. On the Start screen, select the Weather tile if the Weather app isn't open already.

2. In the Weather app, select the Settings button on the app bar. The Settings screen appears, as shown in **Figure 2-13.** Settings is the bottommost option on the app bar. If you have trouble locating it, select the Show Options button, the topmost button on the app bar, to see the buttons on the app bar.

![Weather Settings screen showing General options with Choose a mode (Light, Dark, Windows default selected), Windows color settings link, Show temperature in: Fahrenheit selected / Celsius, and Launch Location options with Default Location selected and San Francisco, CA entered]

FIGURE 2-13

TIP

It may be hard to remember whether you need the Settings panel or the app bar to do something. In general, functions on the app bar are used more frequently than those on the Settings panel. When in doubt, guess — that's how discoveries are made.

3. Choose whether to show air temperatures in Fahrenheit or Celsius.

4. Choose a Launch Location option. The Always Detect My Location option tells the Weather app to note by way of your Internet connection where you are currently and give the weather report for that place. Select Default Location and enter the name of the place where you live if you want to receive weather forecasts for that place.

TIP

Select Privacy Statement in the Settings window if you're interested in how Microsoft collects data about you when you use Weather and other apps made by Microsoft. You see a page clotted with legalese and other obfuscations.

TIP

Changes to settings take effect immediately. You don't have to save or activate your changes.

Search for a Desktop App

1. Open the Start screen: Click the Windows button in the lower-left corner of the desktop or press ⊞.

2. In the Search box (you find it to the right of the Windows button), type **calc** (the first four letters of the word *calculator*). The Search panel appears on the left side of the screen, as shown in **Figure 2-14.** To begin with, the Search panel lists what it thinks are the best matches for the term you entered. You can search for just about anything from the Search box.

Redirect your search

| All | Apps | Documents | Email | Web | More ▾ |

Best match

▦ Calculator
App

Search the web

🔍 calc - See web results   ›

🔍 calc|ulator   ○

FIGURE 2-14

Select a menu item at the top of the Search panel (refer to **Figure 2-14**) to redirect your search. For example, select Documents to search for files on your computer; select Web to search the web. You can select More to open a drop-down menu and search for any number of things, including folders, music files, photos, and videos.

3. Type **ulator** to finish typing the word *calculator*. The Search panel lists only items with the complete word *calculator* in them, including the Calculator app.

4. Select the Calculator app to open it on the desktop, as shown in **Figure 2-15.** To perform a calculation, select the buttons on the screen or use a keyboard.

Calculator

≡ Standard

History   Memory

There's no history yet

0

MC	MR	M+	M-	MS

%	CE	C	⌫
1/x	x^2	$\sqrt[3]{x}$	÷
7	8	9	×
4	5	6	−
1	2	3	+
+/−	0	.	=

FIGURE 2-15

5. Return to the Start screen: Click the Windows button in the lower-left corner of the desktop or press ⊞.

6. Type **calculator** again in the Search box. Again, the Search panel appears, and the Calculator app appears at the top of the Search panel (refer to **Figure 2-14**).

7. Display the context menu on the Calculator app and choose Pin to Start on the context menu, as shown in **Figure 2-16.** (If Unpin from Start appears on the context menu, the Calculator tile is already on the Start screen; disregard this step.) Use one of these techniques to display the context menu:

- **Mouse:** Right-click Calculator in the Search panel.

- **Touchscreen:** Touch and hold Calculator in the Search panel until the context menu appears, and then release your finger.

8. Open the Start screen and note where the Calculator tile appears. You can open the Calculator by selecting this tile.

> To remove a tile from the Start screen, display its context menu and select Unpin from Start.

TIP

FIGURE 2-16

Arrange and Group Apps on the Start Screen

1. You can rearrange tiles on the Start screen by dragging them to different places. On the Start screen, drag the Calculator tile to a different location. As you move the tile, other tiles move out of the way, like a game of Dodge Tile.

2. To start with, the Start screen places tiles in one of two groups: Life at a Glance and Play and Explore. You can find these group names at the top of the start screen. Tap or click the words *Play and Explore* to change the name of the Play and Explore group. A text box appears, as shown in **Figure 2-17.** Enter a new name here (or keep the old name) and press Enter.

Click or tap to change a group name

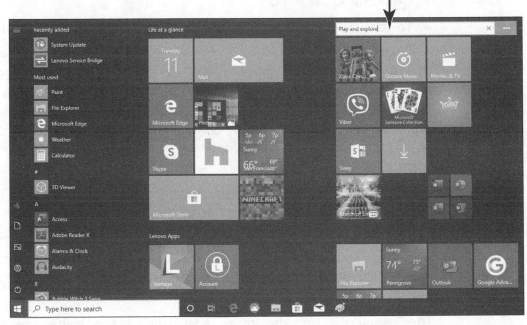

FIGURE 2-17

3. Create a new group for Calculator by dragging the Calculator tile to the lower-right corner of the Start screen so that it's separate from other tiles. Then gently drag the pointer above the Calculator tile. The words *Name group* and two horizontal lines appear after you stop dragging, as shown in **Figure 2-18, top.**

4. Tap or click after you see the two vertical lines. A text box appears, as shown in **Figure 2-18, middle.** You just created a new group with Calculator as the tile.

5. Type a name for the group into the text box, as shown in **Figure 2-18, bottom.** You can change the name at any time by repeating Steps 3 and 4. To remove the name, select the X to the right of the text box. Create groups to organize app tiles on the Start screen.

6. Use one of the following methods to open the context menu on the Calculator tile:

- **Mouse:** Position the pointer over the tile and right-click. (A left click would open the app.)

- **Touchscreen:** Swipe slightly down or up on the tile. (A direct tap would open the app.)

Change the size of the Calculator tile. On the context menu, select Resize and then select the Wide option on the submenu, as shown in **Figure 2-19.** (The options you see on a touchscreen are the same, but are arranged differently on the context menu.) As well as the Wide, Medium, and Small options, Windows 10 provides a Large option for some tiles.

TIP Choose the Large or Wide resize option for apps you use often. The larger the tile, the easier it is to find on the Start screen.

7. Locate a tile on the Start screen that doesn't need to be there. Then select the tile and select Unpin from Start on the context menu to remove the tile from the Start screen. (See Step 6 if you need instructions for displaying the context menu.)

TIP The Start screen becomes more useful and personal when you eliminate tiles that you don't need and arrange tiles to suit your sense of order.

Click or tap to display the text box

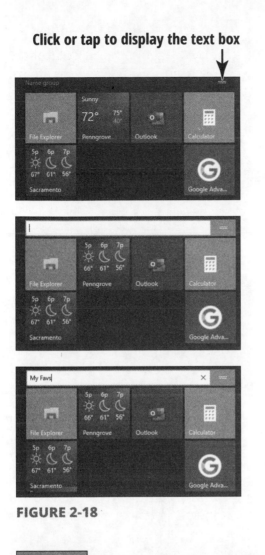

FIGURE 2-18

FIGURE 2-19

Chapter 3

Adjusting Windows 10 Settings

O ut of the box, Windows 10 is showy and colorful. If you don't like that look, however, you can change the photos and colors you see on the screen. Adjusting Windows 10 settings can also make Windows 10 easier and more fun to use. When you're ready, you can dive in and make Windows 10 yours.

In this chapter, you personalize the Lock screen. You see this screen many times a day, so it should please you. You also choose a picture to identify your account on the Start menu. This chapter also explains how to make your screen easier to see and enable features such as Narrator, which reads aloud content from the screen. Finally, you discover how to customize the Start menu and decide which notifications pop up in the lower-right corner of your screen.

Many people leave Windows 10 largely as they found it. Some love to tweak, tinker, and tune. How far you go in personalizing Windows 10 is up to you — it's your computer, after all.

TIP

See Chapter 4 for information on changing passwords and other User settings.

Access the Settings Screen

1. Starting on the desktop, click or tap the Start button (or press the ⊞ key).

2. Choose Settings on the Start menu, as shown in **Figure 3-1** (your Start menu may look different).

TIP

Turn to Chapter 1 if you need help opening an app on the Start menu.

Click or tap to enlarge the Start menu

Choose Settings

FIGURE 3-1

As shown in Figure 3-1, you can click or tap the Options button at the top of the Start menu to enlarge the menu and make it easier to read.

3. The Settings screen appears, as shown in **Figure 3-2.** The Settings screen is the starting point for changing the settings here, there, and everywhere on your computer.

4. One at a time, select each icon in the Settings screen, starting with System, to see the options available. Select the Back button (the square with the left-pointing arrow, located in the upper-left corner of the screen) to return to the Settings screen.

5. On the Settings screen, enter the word **printer** in the Find a Setting box (located at the top of the screen; refer to **Figure 3-2**). As soon as you enter the word, the Settings screen shows you a list of settings that pertain to printers. You can select a setting on the list to open the dialog box where the setting is located.

Search for a setting

FIGURE 3-2

TIP

Windows 10 offers many different settings. Locating them can be a chore. Often the easiest way to find a setting is to enter its name in the Find a Setting box on the Settings screen.

Personalize the Lock Screen

1. On the Settings screen, select Personalization.

2. On the Personalization screen, select Lock Screen. The Lock Screen Preview screen opens, as shown in **Figure 3-3.** On the Background drop-down menu, choose Picture (if it isn't already chosen), as shown in **Figure 3-3.**

TIP

The Lock screen is the first screen you see when you start Windows 10.

See a picture on the Lock screen

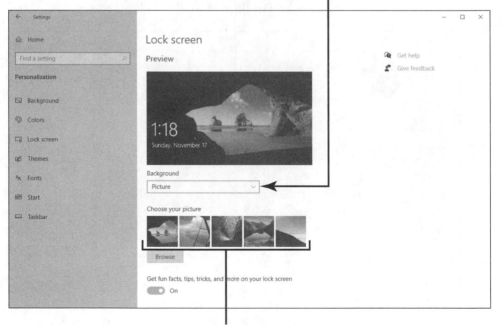

Choose a picture thumbnail

FIGURE 3-3

3. Just above the Browse button, select each thumbnail photo, one at a time. The larger preview photo changes to show the thumbnail you selected. Select a photo that's different from the one you started with. (You can always change it later.)

TIP You can use the Browse button to select one of your own photos from the Pictures folder. See Chapter 10 for information on adding photos to this folder and its subfolders.

TIP Rather than see one image on the start screen, you can see a slide show of images in your Pictures folder. On the Background menu, choose Slideshow.

4. Return to the Start screen. Select your account picture (the topmost icon on the left side of the Start screen). The menu shown in **Figure 3-4** appears. Select Lock on the menu to display the Lock screen.

TIP You can lock your computer anytime by pressing ⊞+L.

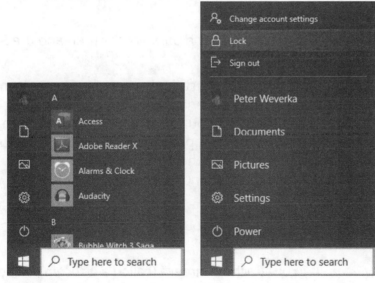

FIGURE 3-4

5. The photo you selected in Step 3 appears on the Lock screen. Display the Password screen as follows:

- **Mouse:** Click anywhere.

- **Touchscreen:** Swipe up.

- **Keyboard:** Press any key on the keyboard.

6. Enter your password, if you have one. The Windows desktop screen appears.

Choose an Account Picture

1. On the Settings screen, select Accounts. See "Access the Settings Screen," earlier in this chapter, if you need help opening the Settings screen. Your current Account picture appears in the Your Info screen, as shown in **Figure 3-5.** (If you haven't selected a picture yet, your picture may just be an outline.)

TIP Your account picture appears on the password screen and the Start screen.

2. To choose one of your photos, select the Browse for One button. The contents of your Pictures folder appears in the Open dialog box. From here, you can select the Up button to access any folder on your computer or select a subfolder to open. When you find the picture you want, select it and then select the Choose Picture button. Or select Cancel to return to the previous screen without changing your account picture.

TIP See Chapter 10 for information about adding photos to your Pictures folder.

3. If you have a built-in or attached camera (called a *webcam*), select the Camera app under Create Your Picture. The Camera app opens with a preview of what your camera sees. See Chapter 10 for information on taking pictures with a webcam.

Your info

PETER WEVERKA

Billing info, family settings, subscriptions, security settings, and more
Manage my Microsoft account

You need to update some info for your Microsoft account.
Update info

Sign in with a local account instead

Create your picture

Camera

Browse for one

Choose a photo

FIGURE 3-5

TIP
You may be able to use another app to select or create a picture. Select the app under Create Your Picture.

4. Return to the Start screen to see your new account picture. To return to the Start screen, click or tap the Start button or press ⊞ on your keyboard.

TIP
The easiest way to access the Accounts screen and change your account picture is through your account name. On the Start screen, select your name and then select Change Account Settings, as shown in **Figure 3-6.** Voilà! The Accounts screen appears, with Your Info selected.

Change your account picture

FIGURE 3-6

Check for Important Updates

1. To check for updates to Windows 10, select Update & Security on the Settings screen. See "Access the Settings Screen," earlier in this chapter, if you need help getting to the PC Settings screen.

2. On the Update & Security screen, select Windows Update. The Windows Update screen appears, as shown in **Figure 3-7.**

3. The Windows Update screen informs you when Windows 10 last checked for updates and whether any were found. Select the Check for Updates button to find out whether any updates are available and update Windows 10 on your computer.

4. For some updates to be installed, your computer has to shut down and restart. In cases like this, you see the Restart Now button on the Windows Update screen. You can select the Restart Now button to install the updates right away or just wait until next time you shut down and restart on your own to install the updates.

TIP

Another way to handle updates is to simply leave your computer on overnight. Windows 10 performs the update as you sleep.

FIGURE 3-7

5. You may see a message that one or more updates will be down-loaded and installed automatically. You do not have to do anything to install these updates — the update process is automatic. Return to the desktop to let Windows 10 manage updates automatically.

You can select the Advanced Options link on the Windows Update screen to choose how Windows 10 installs updates. Select the View Update History button and get a history of updates that Windows 10 has made to your computer.

Installing an update seldom takes more than a few minutes. You can use your system during the update process.

For information on other updates and maintaining Windows 10, see Chapter 12.

Make Windows 10 Easier to Use

1. On the Settings screen, select Ease of Access. (See "Access the Settings Screen" for help.) The Ease of Access screen, shown in **Figure 3-8,** appears. This screen offers many settings to make your computer, mouse, and monitor easier to use. These settings are organized into three categories: Vision, Hearing, and Interaction.

   TIP

   Here's a quick way to open the Ease of Access screen: Press ⊞+U (for *usability*).

2. Under Vision, choose the Display settings (refer to **Figure 3-8**). These settings make the screen easier to view and read. You find settings here for making text larger and brighter.

Settings			— □ ×

⌂ Home

Find a setting 🔍

Ease of Access

Vision

🖵 Display

🐭 Mouse pointer

I Text cursor

🔍 Magnifier

🎨 Color filters

☀ High contrast

🗔 Narrator

Hearing

🔊 Audio

🔲 Closed captions

Display

Make your display easier to see.

Make text bigger

Sample text

Drag the slider until the sample text is easy to read, then click Apply

A |————————————————— A

Apply

Make everything bigger

Change the size of apps and text on the main display

100% (Recommended) ⌄

Change the size of apps and text on other displays

Change the size and color of your cursor and mouse pointer

Make everything brighter

Change the brightness of your built-in display

☀ ————————————●————————— 29 %

Change brightness automatically or use night light

FIGURE 3-8

3. Also under Vision, choose the Mouse Pointer settings to change the size and color of the mouse pointer. As shown in **Figure 3-9,** Windows 10 offers mouse pointers of different sizes and colors. Choose the combination that tickles your fancy.

FIGURE 3-9

4. Also under Vision, choose Text Cursor settings to change the color and thickness of the text cursor. The *text cursor* is the vertical line that appears onscreen to show you where text will appear when you begin to type.

5. Again under Vision, choose Magnifier settings to enlarge what is on your computer screen. These settings are for people who have difficulty seeing. When Magnifier is turned on, the Magnifier toolbar appears onscreen, as shown in **Figure 3-10.** (Click or tap the magnifying glass icon on the taskbar to see this toolbar, if necessary.) Click or tap the plus sign on the Magnifier toolbar to zoom a portion of the screen for easier viewing. Click or tap the minus sign to see the screen at normal size.

TIP

Without turning the Magnifier switch on, you can magnify the screen. Press ⊞ +plus key to zoom in using Magnifier. Press ⊞ +minus key to zoom out using Magnifier.

6. Under Vision, choose a Color Filters setting if you are color blind. If you know which type of color blindness you have — deuteranopia, protanopia, tritanopia — you can choose its name on the Color Filters menu to make seeing items onscreen easier.

Magnifier

Use Magnifier to zoom in on parts of your display. Magnifier can run in full screen, in a separate window, or as a lens that follows your mouse pointer around the screen.

Use Magnifier

Turn on Magnifier

On

FIGURE 3-10

7. Under Vision, choose High Contrast settings to alter the screen in a way that might make seeing text easier. These settings are also for people who have difficulty seeing. After you choose a theme, you can choose a color for text, hyperlinks, disabled text, selected text, button text, and backgrounds. Click Apply after you make your choices. Choose None and click Apply if you want to return to the default Windows 10 contrast settings.

8. Under Vision, choose Narrator settings to have content on the screen read aloud. These settings are for people who have difficulty reading. After turning on the Narrator switch, you choose voice, speed, and pitch settings to determine what the narrator's voice sounds like.

9. Under Hearing, choose Audio Settings to increase the default volume and control whether you hear stereo or mono sound on your computer. If you have poor-quality speakers, turning the Mono Audio option to On can improve the sound.

10. Also under Hearing, choose Closed Captions settings to control how subtitles appear in audio and video presentations. Choose Font settings to describe what you want the text in the captions to look like. Choose Background and Window settings to describe what the box where the captions appear looks like. The Preview box shows what your choices mean in real terms.

11. Under Interaction, choose Speech settings to dictate text instead of typing it and control your computer and device with voice commands.

12. Also under Interaction, choose Keyboard settings to type without using a physical keyboard. This onscreen keyboard uses the layout of a conventional keyboard. However, most people find that the standard Windows 10 virtual keyboard is more flexible. See Chapter 1 for information on the virtual keyboard layouts.

13. Again under Interaction, choose Mouse settings if for some strange reason you want to control the mouse with the keys on the numeric keypad.

Customize the Start Menu

1. On the Settings screen, select Personalization. See "Access the Settings Screen," earlier in this chapter, if you need help opening the Settings screen.

2. On the Personalization screen, select Start. The Start screen opens, as shown in **Figure 3-11.** This screen offers ways to customize the Start menu and the Start screen.

3. Under Start, drag the sliders to On or Off to choose what you want Windows 10 to display on the Start screen and Start menu:

- **Show More Tiles on Start:** Enlarges the Windows 10 Start screen. Choose this option if your Start screen is crowded with app tiles.

- **Show App List in Start Menu:** Places a list of apps installed on your computer on the Start menu. The apps are listed in alphabetical order.

- **Show Recently Added Apps:** Places the names of apps you recently acquired on the Start menu. The names of these apps appear under the "Recently Added" heading.

- **Show Most Used Apps:** Places the names of programs you use most often on the Start menu. The names of these programs appear under the "Most Used" heading.

- **Show Suggestions Occasionally in Start:** Places the names of apps and files on the Start screen that Windows 10 believes you want to see there.

- **Use Start Full Screen:** Makes the Start screen cover the entire desktop, rather than a portion of the desktop.

FIGURE 3-11

- **Show Recently Opened Items in Jump Lists on Start or the Taskbar and in File Explorer Quick Access:** Allows you to quickly open folders, files, and windows from the Start menu, taskbar, and File Explorer screen. When you move the pointer over an app or program on the Start menu, an arrow appears; select the arrow to see a menu of items you can open. When you move the pointer over an icon on the taskbar, thumbnail windows appear so that you can choose which window to open. In File Explorer, the items are listed in the Quick Access section of the navigation pane.

Handle Notifications

1. *Notifications* are the sometimes pesky little message boxes that appear in the lower-right corner of the screen when you least expect them. You can decide for yourself whether notifications appear and which notifications you want to see. On the Settings screen, select System. See "Access the Settings Screen," earlier in this chapter, if you need help opening the Settings screen.

2. Select Notifications & Actions to see the screen shown in **Figure 3-12.** The top of this screen is for customizing the Quick Actions panel. Scroll past Quick Actions options to see the options for customizing how and when notifications appear.

3. Under Notifications in the Notification & Actions screen, turn options on or off to tell Windows whether you want notifications to appear on your screen.

4. Scroll down the Notification & Actions screen to the area called Show Notifications from These Senders. You see an alphabetical list of apps that can deliver notifications. Drag the On/Off sliders to tell Windows 10 which applications you want to deliver notifications.

5. Select the Close button (the X) to close the Settings window.

FIGURE 3-12

Chapter **4**

Working with User Accounts

Windows 10 seeks an Internet connection automatically from the moment you start it. More often than not, you connect to the Internet using a wireless or *Wi-Fi* connection. For this reason, if you start a laptop or tablet in a coffee shop or library, you may see a notification that one or more network connections are available. That's convenient.

A computer without an Internet connection is an island, if not a paperweight. Connecting to a network, however, opens a door to your computer — and malefactors try to push through that door to access your computer. Windows 10 has a *firewall* that monitors and restricts traffic in and out. Don't be afraid of connecting to the Internet, but be aware of the risks and be careful to connect to a network that seems trustworthy. In Chapter 1, you create a local user account. You need a Microsoft Account to take full advantage of Windows 10 features such as the Microsoft Store for apps (see Chapter 9), OneDrive for online storage (see Chapter 15), and synchronized settings between computers. In this chapter, you create a Microsoft Account and choose a secure method for logging in to your account. You also discover how to switch to Airplane mode, create a local account, and switch from a local account to a Microsoft Account. To control access to your computer, you find out how to use a password to unlock your computer.

If other people use your computer, you may want to create more than one local account. When each person who uses your computer has a separate account, you can keep data, apps, and settings tidy and private. I recommend having only one administrator account for each computer.

Even if you're the only one using your computer, you may want more than one account. For example, if you create a local account, you can experiment with the new account — changing the look and function of Windows 10 — without affecting your first account.

Many of the steps in this chapter involve entering text, such as your name. If you don't have a physical keyboard, use the virtual keyboard, which is covered in Chapter 1.

Connect to the Internet

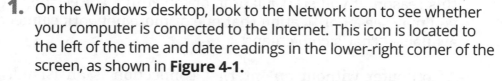

1. On the Windows desktop, look to the Network icon to see whether your computer is connected to the Internet. This icon is located to the left of the time and date readings in the lower-right corner of the screen, as shown in **Figure 4-1.**

Select or choose options by moving the mouse pointer and left-clicking or by tapping a touchscreen with your finger.

2. Select the Network icon. The Networks panel appears on the right side of your screen, as shown in **Figure 4-2 (left),** and lists all available network connections. There may be no connections or dozens.

If you see *Not connected* and *No connections available,* you may be out of luck. Check your computer documentation to see whether your PC has wireless capability and whether you need to turn on a mechanical switch.

Network Connection icon

FIGURE 4-1

TIP

If your computer is near a router (DSL or cable) and you don't have wireless capability, you may be able to connect your PC and the router using an Ethernet cable, which is thicker than a phone line, with wider connections.

3. Select a connection. Note that not all displayed connections are accessible or desirable.

TIP

If you're not sure that you can trust a connection, you might want to forego a connection — better safe than sorry. (Unsafe wireless connections can be used to eavesdrop on your activities, though that scenario is rare.) However, if an available connection sports the name of the establishment you're in or near, such as a restaurant or a coffee shop, the connection may be safe. The same is true of connections at libraries, airports, and many other public spaces.

Available wireless connections   **Connect automatically next time**

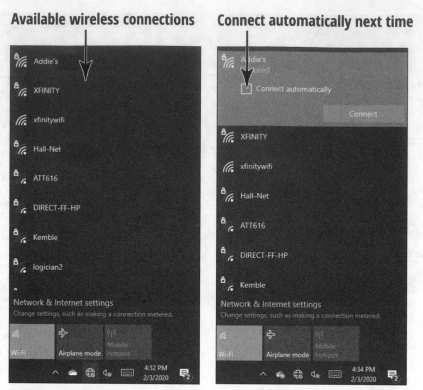

FIGURE 4-2

4. After you select a connection, the selected tile expands and displays the Connect Automatically check box, as shown in **Figure 4-2 (right).** If you trust the connection and might want to use it again, select the check box. Otherwise, deselect the check box. To continue, select the Connect button.

5. You may be prompted to enter a network security key (a series of characters), which limits access to those who know the key. See **Figure 4-3.** The key protects that network and its users. If you're using a hotel's connection, you can obtain the key from the front desk. If you don't know the key, select Cancel. Otherwise, enter the key (dots appear as you type) and select Next.

TIP

If the connection is public and open, you won't be prompted for a key. Open connections are common in libraries, coffee shops, and other places many people come and go.

A secure network requires a key

FIGURE 4-3

6. If you entered the correct key or none was required, you may see this message: *Do you want to turn on sharing between PCs and connect to devices on this network?* The term *sharing* refers to allowing computers access to your files or to a device, such as a printer. You should share at home but not in a public location. Choose one of the following:

   • **No:** This option prevents you from connecting directly with other computers and protects your computer from networks in public places. You'll still have Internet access.

   • **Yes:** This option enables you to share documents and devices between your computers on a home or office network.

TIP

If you're not sure about which option to choose, go with No.

7. When a Wi-Fi connection is established, the word *Connected* appears next to the network name in the Networks panel, as shown in **Figure 4-4.** The connection name and signal strength appear as well. The connection strength (but not the name) appears next to the time and date in the notification area in the lower-right corner of the screen (see **Figure 4-4**).

TIP

If you selected the Connect Automatically check box (in Step 4), the connection will be used anytime it is available. If you move your computer to another location out of range of this network (usually a few hundred yards), you will have to repeat these steps to connect to another network.

Select to disconnect

Connection status

Ad...e's
Connected, secured

Properties

Disconnect

XFINITY

xfinitywifi

Hall-Net

ATT616

DIRECT-FF-HP

Kemble

Network & Internet settings
Change settings, such as making a connection metered.

Wi-Fi | Airplane mode | Mobile hotspot

4:54 PM
2/3/2020

Signal strength

FIGURE 4-4

Disconnect (or Switch to Airplane Mode)

1. When you shut down your computer or move your computer far
   enough away from the connection, your computer disconnects from
   the Internet automatically. Suppose you want to disconnect on your
   own? To disconnect your computer from the Internet, display the
   Networks panel again (refer to **Figure 4-4**).

2. Select the Disconnect button. (If you disconnect your computer,
   reconnect before continuing to Step 3.)

3. For safety's sake, airlines don't want passengers to send or receive wireless data signals while the airplane is in flight; these signals can interfere with the airplane's communications systems. This is why the captain gives the order to "turn off all electrical devices." Rather than turn off your computer, however, you can switch to Airplane mode. To do so, open the Networks panel and select the Airplane Mode button. This button is located at the bottom of the Networks panel.

4. In Airplane mode, an airplane icon appears to the left of the time and date readings in the lower-right corner of the screen, as shown in **Figure 4-5.** Your computer doesn't send wireless data signals in Airplane mode. To switch out of Airplane mode and reconnect to the Internet, select the airplane icon to display the Network panel. Then select the Airplane Mode button (refer to **Figure 4-5**).

Airplane icon

Select to leave Airplane mode

FIGURE 4-5

Switching to Airplane mode is much more convenient than turning off your computer's network connection and turning it back on again. It takes but a second or two.

Create a New Microsoft Account

1. On the Start screen, select your picture on the left side of the screen. In the pop-up menu that appears, choose Change Account Settings, as shown in **Figure 4-6.** The Settings app opens to the Accounts screen. Your account information appears with the words *Local Account* under your name, as shown in **Figure 4-7.**

TIP

If you see don't see *Local Account*, you already have a Microsoft Account and don't need to follow these steps.

Select for fast access to Accounts screen

FIGURE 4-6

Settings

Home

Find a setting

Accounts

Your info

Email & accounts

Sign-in options

Access work or school

Sync your settings

Your info

BILLY
Local Account

Windows is better when your settings and files automatically sync. Use a Microsoft account to easily get all your stuff on all your devices.

Sign in with a Microsoft account instead

Create your picture

Camera

Browse for one

Help from the web

Creating a Microsoft account

Logging in to your Microsoft account

Get help

Give feedback

FIGURE 4-7

2. Select the Sign In with a Microsoft Account Instead link. The Sign In screen appears. To create a new account, select the Create One! link.

3. On the Create Account screen, create the account with an email address or a phone number. Messages about your Microsoft Account will be sent to the email address or phone number you enter.

- **Email address:** Type the email address you want to use for this account in the Email Address box and select Next.

- **Phone Number:** Select the Use a Phone Number Instead link. Then enter your phone number and select Next.

4. In the Create a Password box, type a password. Dots appear instead of what you type. Use at least eight characters, including at least two uppercase letters, two lowercase letters, two numbers, or two symbols. No spaces are allowed.

TIP

Your password should be easy enough for you to remember and type, but not easy for someone else to guess. Don't use the names of any family members (including pets). A good password can be difficult to create, so try this trick: Think of a memorable phrase or lyric. Next, use the first letter from each word, capitalizing some of those letters. Then substitute some letters with numbers (for example, 3 for the letter *E* or the number 0 for the letter *O*). Don't put your password on a sticky note near your screen.

5. Enter your first and last name; then select Next.

6. In the What's Your Birth Date? screen (see **Figure 4-8**), enter your country or region if it is not already selected.

7. Select the month, day, and year of your birth. (You can lie, but be sure to remember your response.)

8. Review your entries and select the Next button.

9. On the Verify screen, enter the code Microsoft sent to the email address or phone number you entered in Step 3.

10. Select the Next button. The Sign In to This Device Using Your Microsoft Account screen appears. Enter the user name and password to your local account, if you had a password. Then click Next. Congratulations! You just created a Microsoft Account.

FIGURE 4-8

Create a Local Account

1. "Local account" is Microsoft's name for your ability to start your computer without signing in to Microsoft. Before you create or sign in with a local account, save your work. Then select the Start button, select your picture on the Start menu, and in the pop-up menu that appears (refer to **Figure 4-6**), choose Change Account Settings. You see the Accounts screen. If you see the words *Local Account* on this screen, you're already signed in with a local account.

TIP

You can't download and install apps from the Microsoft Store without signing in with a Microsoft Account. Nor can you upload files to OneDrive. So why have a local account? If you're concerned about privacy and security, if you don't want Microsoft to peer over your shoulder and track your every move when you use your computer, consider creating a local account. You can always switch to your Microsoft Account when you want to install apps from the Microsoft Store, use OneDrive, or use Skype (see "Switch from a Local to an Existing Microsoft Account," later in this chapter).

TIP

To create a local account for someone else to use your computer, see "Create a Local Account for Someone in Your Household," later in this chapter.

2. Choose the Sign In with a Local Account Instead link. You see the Are You Sure screen, shown in **Figure 4-9.** Select the Next button.

3. Enter the password of your Microsoft Account in the Making Sure It's You screen (refer to **Figure 4-9**) and select OK.

4. In the next screen, shown in **Figure 4-10,** enter a user name, a password (twice), and a word or two to jar your memory if you forget your password; then select Next.

TIP

Passwords are case sensitive. In other words, your computer recognizes uppercase letters and lowercase letters when you create and enter a password. Remember which letters in your password are upper- and lowercase.

Are you sure you want to switch to a local account?

Windows works better when you sign in with Microsoft. Switching to a local account means you won't see your personalized settings on all your devices, and you might be asked to sign in again if you want to access info associated with your account.

If you still want to continue, go to the next step to verify your identity.

Pete

peter

Windows Security   ×

Making sure it's you

For security, Windows needs to verify your identity

Peter

Password

MicrosoftAccount\pete@mail.com

OK   Cancel

Next   Cancel

FIGURE 4-9

← Enter your local account info

Enter the user name and password for your new or existing local account. This is the account you'll use to sign in to Windows from now on.

If you want to continue to sign in to Windows with Windows Hello, you'll need to set up a password.

User name   peter   ✕

New password

Confirm password

Password hint

Next   Cancel

FIGURE 4-10

TIP

If you want to sign in to your local account without having to enter a password, leave the Password, Reenter Password, and Password Hint text boxes blank. Later in this chapter, the sections "Create a Password for a Local Account" and "Change or Remove a Local Account Password" explain the ins and outs of local account passwords.

5. Select the Sign Out and Finish button. Your Microsoft Account closes, Windows restarts, and you see the Windows 10 screen.

6. Enter the password you created in Step 3. When you start your computer, Windows 10 assumes that you want to sign in with the account you were using when you last shut down your computer. If you shut down when signed in with your local account, you are asked to provide the password for your local account the next time you start your computer.

TIP

When you start a computer with more than one account, account names appear in the lower-left corner of the Windows 10 screen. Select an account name in the lower-left corner to tell Windows which account to open.

Switch from a Local to an Existing Microsoft Account

1. Follow these steps to sign in with your Microsoft Account when you are currently signed in with your local account. On the Start screen, select your name in the upper-left corner of the screen and then choose Change Account Settings from the pop-up menu that appears (refer to **Figure 4-6**). The Accounts screen opens. Your account information appears with *Local Account* under your name (refer to **Figure 4-7**).

TIP

If you don't have a Microsoft Account already, see "Create a New Microsoft Account," earlier in this chapter.

TIP

If you don't see *Local Account* under your user account name, you're already signed in with your Microsoft Account.

2. Select the Sign In with a Microsoft Account Instead link. The screen shown in **Figure 4-11** appears. Type the email address or phone number of your Microsoft Account and select the Next button.

![Microsoft account sign-in screen]

Microsoft account   ✕

Microsoft

Sign in

Email, phone, or Skype

No account? Create one!

Forgot username

Next

Terms of use   Privacy & cookies   ...

FIGURE 4-11

3. Enter the password of your Microsoft Account and select the Sign In button.

4. In the Current Windows Password text box, enter the password of your local account and select the Next button, as shown in **Figure 4-12.** The Accounts screen opens, where you see the user name and email address of your Microsoft account.

Microsoft account ✕

■■ Microsoft

peterwev@gmail.com

Sign into this computer using your Microsoft account

Next time you sign into this computer, use your Microsoft account password or Windows Hello, if you've set it up.
We'll need your current Windows password one last time.

•••••••••••

Next

Terms of use   Privacy & cookies   •••

FIGURE 4-12

Create a Local Account for Someone in Your Household

1. Consider creating a local account for each person who uses your computer. A local account is more than just a way to sign in. Each local account preserves the user's settings and Internet browsing history. When you set up a local account, Windows 10 creates separate folders called Documents, Pictures, Videos, and Music for the account holder. Only the account holder can open and edit files in these special folders. To create a local account, select your name on the Start screen and choose Change Account Settings on the menu that appears (refer to **Figure 4-6**). The Settings app opens to the Accounts screen.

TIP

To create a local account, you must be your computer's administrator. To see whether you're the administrator, look for the word *Administrator* below your name on the Your Info page of the Settings screen.

2. On the left, select Family & Other Users. On the right, select Add Someone Else to This PC. The How Will This Person Sign In screen appears.

3. At the bottom of the How Will This Person Sign In screen, select the link called I Don't Have This Person's Sign-In Information.

TIP

If you know you want a Microsoft Account instead of a local account, jump to "Create a New Microsoft Account" or "Switch from a Local to an Existing Microsoft Account," earlier in this chapter.

4. On the next screen, select Add a User without a Microsoft Account.

5. On the next screen (it's called Create a User for This PC), enter the user name in the first box, as shown in **Figure 4-13.** Use the person's first name, last name, first and last name, initials, or nickname — something easy to remember and type.

TIP

You are not required to use a password with a local account, which makes signing in easy. However, without a password, anyone can use the computer and access information that you might want to protect.

Microsoft account   ✕

Create a user for this PC

If you want to use a password, choose something that will be easy for you to remember but hard for others to guess.

Who's going to use this PC?

| Dobbs   ✕ |

Make it secure.

| ••••• |

| ••••• |

In case you forget your password

| What was your first pet's name?   ⌄ |

| Spot |

| What's the name of the city where you were born?   ⌄ |

| Hemet |

| What was your childhood nickname?   ⌄ |

| Quirky |

                                        Next   Back

FIGURE 4-13

6. In the Password box, enter a password (or skip to Step 9 if you don't care to create a password for your account). A dot will appear for each character you type.

TIP

For suggestions on creating a good password, see the tip in Step 4 in the section, "Create a New Microsoft Account," earlier in this chapter.

7. In the Reenter Password box, type the same password exactly.

8. In the three drop-down menus, choose a security question and type the answer in the text box. If you forgot your password, you will be able to recover it by answering a security question correctly.

9. After completing all the available boxes, choose the Next button. In the Accounts screen, the new user name appears under Other Users, as shown in **Figure 4-14.**

![Settings window showing Family & other users page. Left panel: Home, Find a setting, Accounts, Your info, Email & accounts, Sign-in options, Access work or school, Family & other users, Sync your settings. Main panel: Your family section with "Add a family member", Other users section with "Add someone else to this PC" and "Dobbs Local account". Right panel: Help from the web, Switching users, Setting screen time limits, Creating a local user account, Get help, Give feedback. An arrow points to Dobbs labeled "The new user name".]

The new user name

FIGURE 4-14

10. Return to the Start screen and select your user name. Notice that the new user name appears on the drop-down menu. You can switch between accounts by selecting a user name on the drop-down menu. To sign out of an account, choose Sign Out.

11. In the drop-down menu, select the new user name to switch to that account.

12. A screen appears with the new user name. If you used a password on the new user account, type that password in the box and select the onscreen right arrow or press Enter. If you didn't use a password, select the Sign In button.

TIP

The first time you sign in as a new user, you have to wait a moment while apps are installed for the new user. Soon the generic Start screen appears. (Any settings you changed in your account do not transfer to other accounts.)

TIP

When you start a computer for which you've created more than one user account, the users' names appear in the lower-left corner of the Windows 10 screen. To tell Windows which user to sign in with, select a user name on the Windows 10 screen before signing in.

Create a Password for a Local Account

1. If necessary, sign in to the local account that needs a password. On the Start screen, select your name. From the drop-down menu that appears, choose Change Account Settings (refer to **Figure 4-6**). The Settings app opens to the Accounts screen.

TIP

If you already have a password, see the "Change or Remove a Local Account Password," later in this chapter.

2. On the left, select Sign-in Options.

3. In the middle of the screen, select Password.

4. If you don't have a password but want one, select the Add button under Password.

The buttons available under Sign-in Options depend on your current setup. You may see buttons that enable you to create, change, or remove a particular setting.

5. In the Create a Password screen, shown in **Figure 4-15,** enter a password in the New Password box.

For a local account, the password can be any length. See Step 4 in the "Create a New Microsoft Account" section for suggestions about creating a good password.

6. In the Reenter Password box, enter the password again.

7. Enter a hint to remind yourself — and no one else — about your password. And whatever you do, don't include the password in the hint.

8. Select Finish. If any error messages appear, correct the entries and select Next again.

Create a password

New password

Confirm password

Password hint

Next   Cancel

FIGURE 4-15

Change or Remove a Local Account Password

1. If you haven't done so already, sign in to the local account with the password you want to change or remove. On the Start screen, select your name and then choose Change Account Settings. On the left side of the Accounts screen, select Sign-in Options.

2. In the middle of the screen, select Password.

3. Select the Change button.

   If you don't have a password but want one, see the preceding "Create a Password for a Local Account" section.

4. On the Change Your Password screen, enter your current password and then select the Next button.

5. On the next Change Your Password screen (see **Figure 4-16**), enter the new password. (If you don't care to have a password, select Next and skip to Step 8.)

   To remove your current password and use no password, leave all boxes blank. However, especially if you have a laptop that you carry with you, going without a password isn't recommended. Without a password to safeguard it, anyone can get into your laptop.

6. In the Reenter Password box, enter the password again.

7. Enter a hint to remind yourself — and no one else — about your password. Then select Next. If any error messages appear, correct the entries and select Next again.

8. The final screen indicates that you must use your new password the next time you sign in. (This message appears even if you left the password blank, in which case you won't need any password.) Select Finish.

If you don't want a password, leave these boxes blank

FIGURE 4-16

Delete a Local Account

1. Before you delete a local account, make sure that the user of that account is signed out. Moreover, you must be signed in to a Microsoft Account to delete a local account.

2. Select your name on the Start screen and choose Change Account Settings. You land in the Your Info page of the Settings screen. Does it say "administrator" under your name? I hope so, because you must be your computer's administrator to delete a local account. On the Accounts screen, select Family & Other Users.

3. Select the account you want to delete and then select the Remove button, as shown in **Figure 4-17.**

4. In the Delete Account and Data window, select the Delete Account and Data button.

TIP

Take heed of the onscreen warning. Deleting a user account removes the user's data, including all documents, music, and other files. If you're not sure which option is best, choose Cancel.

FIGURE 4-17

Chapter **5**

Getting Comfortable with the Desktop

The *desktop* is Grand Central Station as far as Windows 10 is concerned. Sure, you can open applications from the Start screen (Chapter 2 explains how), but with a few simple modifications, you can open applications from the desktop as well. When you're running more than one application, you can go to the desktop and quickly switch from one application to another. In fact, in Windows 10, you can create a second "virtual" desktop for one set of open applications (applications that pertain to leisure, let's say), and when the boss isn't looking, you can switch to the second desktop to play games or chat with friends.

One key feature of the desktop is the *taskbar,* a strip along the bottom of the screen that shows icons for desktop programs. The taskbar can be used to run and switch between desktop programs. Most programs on the desktop run in windows, as opposed to the full-screen nature of Windows 10 apps.

In this chapter, you get acquainted with the desktop, the taskbar, and windowed apps. You change the date, time, and time zone, as needed.

You resize and reposition windowed apps, and discover how to "add a desktop" for a second set of open applications. You select a background for the desktop and make some desktop apps more convenient to use by pinning them to the taskbar. Finally, you work with the Task Manager, which lets you end any app — desktop or Windows 10.

The desktop originated when using the mouse was the most common method for selecting objects (touchscreens were nonexistent). Therefore, on the desktop, a few tasks are easier to do with the mouse than with touch or a keyboard.

This chapter is an introduction to the desktop. See Part 4 to dive a little deeper into desktop functions, such as organizing documents.

Check Out the Desktop

1. Go to the desktop (if you aren't already there) by using one of these techniques:

- With the Start screen open, display the desktop simply by clicking or tapping the Windows button (it's located in the lower-left corner of your computer screen).

- Press ⊞+D.

- Right-click the Windows button and choose Desktop on the pop-up menu that appears.

2. Your desktop has a picture in the background. Examine your desktop for *icons* — small pictures that represent either programs, which perform functions, or documents, such as letters and photos. You select an icon to run a program or open a document. The Windows 10 desktop displays an icon for the Recycle Bin, where deleted documents go. The Recycle Bin may be the only icon on your desktop, or you may see others. See Chapter 14 for information on using the Recycle Bin.

3. The area at the bottom of the screen is the *taskbar,* shown in **Figure 5-1.** From left to right, the taskbar offers these amenities:

- **Windows button:** Selecting this button opens the Start screen. (Click or tap the button a second time to close the Start screen.)

- **Search box:** You can enter a search term here to look for Windows settings, applications, files on your computer, and information on the Internet.

- **Task View button:** Selecting this button brings up thumbnail images of applications currently running on your computer. You can select an application thumbnail to switch to an application. You can also select New Desktop to open a second desktop (see "Open a Second Desktop," later in this chapter, for more information).

- **Icons:** Some icons appear on the taskbar automatically. Very likely, your taskbar has icons for File Explorer and Edge. You can select these icons to open File Explorer and Edge. When you open an application, Windows 10 places its icon on the taskbar.

- **Icon tray:** The *icon tray* displays icons for programs that run automatically when your computer starts. The date and time are to the right of the icon tray. On the right side of the icon tray is the Notification icon.

TIP You can use the taskbar to switch among programs by selecting the icon for the program you want to use.

4. Select an icon on the taskbar to open the associated program. (Refer to **Figure 5-1** if you aren't sure where the taskbar is located.)

TIP You select items on the desktop or in the taskbar by clicking with the mouse or tapping the touchscreen. To some extent, you can use the Tab and arrow keys, but that's an awkward method.

TIP If you have a touchscreen, note the taskbar icon for the virtual keyboard. See Chapter 1 for information about using the keyboard.

5. Right-click over an icon or tap and hold until a small box appears, and then release. A *context menu* appears with options specific to the icon you selected, as shown in **Figure 5-2.** Select anywhere else on the desktop to dismiss this menu. Repeat this on a few different areas of the screen to see how the context menu changes.

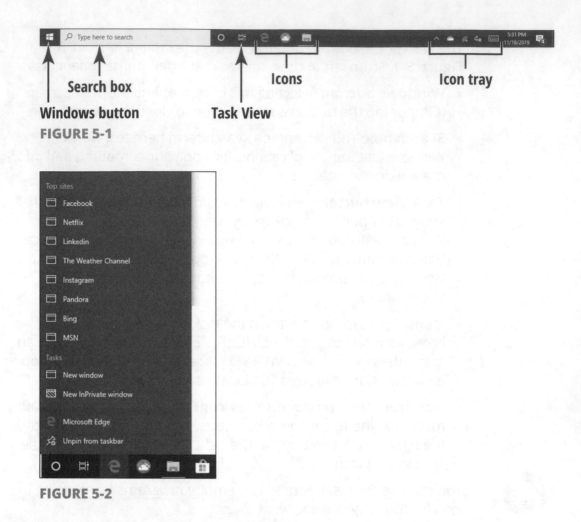

Windows button   **Search box**   **Task View**   **Icons**   **Icon tray**

FIGURE 5-1

FIGURE 5-2

Change the Date or Time

1. Select the date and time displayed in the taskbar. A calendar and clock pop up, as shown in **Figure 5-3.**

TIP

Selecting the date and time on the taskbar also brings up an agenda list from the Calendar. Chapter 8 describes the Calendar in tedious detail. You can click or tap the Hide Agenda button to hide the agenda list.

2. If the date or time is incorrect for your location, select the Windows button and then select the Settings button on the left side of the Start screen. The Settings screen opens. Select Time & Language. You see the Date & Time window, shown in **Figure 5-4, left.**

FIGURE 5-3

3. Windows 10 determines the correct time and date from the Internet, and your computer should show the right time and date, but if it doesn't, turn off the Set Time Automatically option and select the Change button. You see the Change Date and Time screen (see **Figure 5-4**). Select the correct date and time in this screen. Change the time by using the little triangles that point up (later) or down (earlier) or by entering the specific hours and minutes. Select Change to keep your change or Cancel to ignore your change.

4. Back in the Date and Time window, select your Time Zone from the drop-down list, if necessary. Turn the Adjust for Daylight Saving Time option on or off as appropriate.

5. To change the format with which the time and date are displayed in the lower-right corner of the screen, select the Date, Time & Regional Formatting link in the Date & Time window. Then, in the Region window, select the Change Data Formats link. You see the Change Data Formats window (see **Figure 5-5**). Choose how you want the date and time to be displayed on your computer screen.

Turn off automatic time **Select your time zone** **Set the time**

FIGURE 5-4

FIGURE 5-5

Explore the Parts of a Window

1. In the taskbar, select the File Explorer icon (it looks like a folder). File Explorer opens, as shown in **Figure 5-6.**

TIP

File Explorer enables you to view your computer storage, such as hard drives, and folders, which are used to organize your documents. See Chapter 14 for information on using File Explorer.

2. Explore the example window in **Figure 5-6,** starting at the top left:

- **Quick Access toolbar:** The *Quick Access toolbar* gives you fast access to common operations, such as creating a new folder. This toolbar is not present in all windows and may feature different functions, depending on the window.

- **Title bar:** The *title bar,* which is the top line of the window, lists the name of the file or folder that is currently open.

TIP

The title of the window in **Figure 5-6** is This PC, the location File Explorer is focused on when you open File Explorer.

- **Minimize:** The *Minimize button,* located in the upper-right corner of the window, shrinks or hides the window's contents. The program that the window contains is still running and open, but the window is out of sight. You'll still see the program's icon in the taskbar. Select the Minimize button when you want to ignore a particular window but aren't actually done with it. To restore the window, select its icon in the taskbar.

- **Maximize/Restore:** The *Maximize button* (the button with a single square in the upper-right corner of the window) fills the screen with the contents of the window. Select the Maximize button to hide the desktop and other open windows, to concentrate on one window, and to see as much of the window's contents as you can. The *Restore button* (the button with two squares in the upper-right corner) is the name of the button that appears after you select the Maximize button; it replaces the Maximize button. Select the Restore button to return the window to its previous size, which is between maximized and minimized. (Press ⊞+up-arrow key to maximize, and ⊞+down-arrow key to restore or minimize.)

- **Close:** The *Close button* is the button with the X in the upper-right corner of the window. Select the Close button when you are done with the window. Close is also called Quit and Exit. (Press Alt+F4 to close the current window or the desktop itself. This keyboard shortcut works for Windows 10 apps, as well.)

- **Ribbon:** The *Ribbon* is a toolbar that provides access to many functions organized as groups within tabs. The tabs appear across the top of the Ribbon. The first time you run File Explorer, the Ribbon is hidden (collapsed). Display the Ribbon by selecting the caret symbol (^) on the far right, next to Help (the question mark). Select the caret again to hide the Ribbon. You can also press Ctrl+F1 to toggle the Ribbon on and off. (Leave the Ribbon visible for this chapter.) The tabs remain in view and function the same. Although Ribbons vary between programs, most Ribbons have File and View tabs. To use a tab, select its name to display its functions, and then select the item you want to use.

TIP

The Ribbon can help you discover new functions.

- **Contents:** The bulk of the window contains the program or document you're using. File Explorer displays locations on the left and objects in that location on the right.

- **Status bar:** Along the bottom edge of the window, some programs display information about the window or its contents in a single-line *status bar.* File Explorer lists how many files are in the currently open folder and how many files (if any) have been selected.

TIP

Scan the edges of windows. Often, important information and functions are pushed to these edges around the main content area.

3. Select the Close button (the X) to close File Explorer.

TIP

Although the Quick Access toolbar and the Close button work on a touchscreen, they are small targets. You may find a stylus more accurate when dealing with smaller elements.

TIP

See Chapter 2 for information on finding other desktop programs, such as the Calculator.

Quick Access toolbar   **File Explorer window**   **Ribbon**

Status bar

FIGURE 5-6

Resize a Window

1. To resize a window, open File Explorer by selecting the folder icon in the taskbar. (Refer to **Figure 5-6.**)

2. If the window is maximized (fills the screen), select the Restore button to make the window smaller.

3. Use one of these methods to resize the window:

- **Mouse:** Move the mouse pointer to the right edge of the window until the pointer changes to a double-headed arrow, called the *resize pointer*. Click and drag the edge of the window, using the resize pointer. (To drag, click and hold down the mouse button while you move the mouse.)

- **Touchscreen:** Drag the right edge of the window.

Drag left to shrink the window and right to expand it.

TIP

4. Resize the window's width and height at the same time by dragging a corner of the window. If you want a challenge, try resizing the top-right corner without accidentally selecting the Close button.

5. Resize the window's width *or* height by dragging any of the four sides.

You may want to resize a window to show only what you need to see, nothing more. Practice resizing from any side or corner.

TIP

6. Leave the window open as you go on to the next task.

Arrange Some Windows

1. On the desktop, select and open the Recycle Bin by double-clicking or double-tapping its icon. The Recycle Bin contains deleted files and folders. It appears in another File Explorer window. See **Figure 5-7.**

Double-click by clicking the left mouse button twice, without a pause. Double-tap by tapping twice in quick succession.

TIP

2. If File Explorer isn't still open from the preceding section, open it by selecting the folder icon in the taskbar. You now see two overlapping windows on the desktop (refer to **Figure 5-7**), one titled *This PC* and the other titled *Recycle Bin.*

The window in front of the others is called the *active* window. All other windows are *inactive.* Selecting anywhere in an inactive window makes it active and moves it to the front of the others.

TIP

3. Drag the Recycle Bin title bar (avoiding the buttons on the left and right ends) to move that window a little.

4. Drag the This PC title bar (again, avoiding the buttons on both ends). The This PC window moves in front of the Recycle Bin as you move it. Move both windows so that you can see a little of each (refer to **Figure 5-7**).

5. Practice moving both windows. Arranging windows helps you see and do more than one thing at a time. Use the techniques from the preceding section, "Resize a Window," to see as much as you can of both windows at one time.

TIP

If you can't see the title bar of the window you want to move, move the other window to uncover the hidden title bar.

6. Leave both windows open for the following task.

Move a window by dragging its title bar

FIGURE 5-7

Snap a Window

1. Drag one of the windows you worked with in the preceding section to the left edge of the screen. When the mouse pointer or your finger reaches the left edge of the screen, you see an outline on the screen, as shown in **Figure 5-8.** When you release the mouse or your finger, the window resizes automatically to fill the left half of the screen, as shown in **Figure 5-9.** This procedure is called *snap*. (To snap a window using the keyboard, press +left arrow to snap a window to the left; press +right arrow to snap a window to the right.)

Drag the window to the left   **Note the outline**

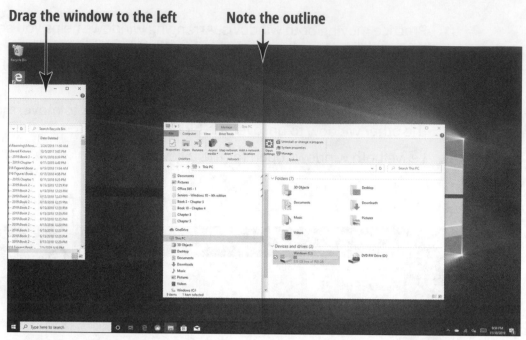

FIGURE 5-8

2. After you snap the first open window, the second open window appears in thumbnail form (see **Figure 5-9**). Tap or click this second window thumbnail to make it fill, or snap to, the right side of the window.

TIP

When two or more windows are displayed side by side like this, they are called *tiled* windows.

3. Drag either window by the title bar away from the edge of the screen. The window returns to its previous size.

4. Drag the window you moved in Step 3 to the upper-right corner of the window. When the mouse pointer or your finger touches the corner of the screen, you see an outline on the screen, but this time the outline occupies the upper-right corner of the screen. And guess what? When you release the mouse pointer or your finger, the window snaps to the upper-right quadrant of the screen. In this way, by snapping windows to the corner of the screen, you can tile four windows on your screen, not two windows.

FIGURE 5-9

TIP

> You can maximize a window by dragging it to the top edge of the screen. Dragging a window to the top is the equivalent of selecting the Maximize button (see the section "Explore the Parts of a Window," earlier in this chapter).

5. Drag the title bar of each open window away from the side of the screen so that neither window is "snapped." You'll need these open windows if you want to move on to "Open a Second Desktop," the next topic in this chapter.

Open a Second Desktop

1. If File Explorer and Recycle Bin aren't open on your desktop (because you didn't follow the previous exercise in this chapter), open those programs now.

2. Select the Task View button on the taskbar. As Chapter 2 explains, you can use this button to switch between open application windows. After you select the Task View button, thumbnail versions of open windows appear on the desktop. At this point, you can select a thumbnail to go to a different application, but don't do that just yet.

TIP

You can press ⊞+Tab to select the Task View button.

3. Notice the New Desktop button that appears after you select the Task View button. This button is located in the upper-left corner of the screen. Select the New Desktop button now. As shown in **Figure 5-10,** two desktop tiles appear at the top of the screen. The desktop tiles are labeled "Desktop 1" and "Desktop 2."

TIP

After you click the New Desktop button, a *timeline* (Microsoft's word) of files and web pages you viewed or opened in the past appears on the right side of the screen (refer to **Figure 5-10**). You can scroll on the timeline to see thumbnail images of files you worked on and web pages you visited. To revisit one of these items, select its thumbnail.

4. Select Desktop 2. You see a brand-new, pristine desktop. Congratulations; you are now in Desktop 2. Create a second (or third or fourth) desktop when you want to keep the first desktop from getting crowded with too many applications or to better organize your work. For example, if you're using applications for your work and using other applications for leisure purposes, put the work applications on one desktop and the leisure applications on another. This will help you find the application you want to work with.

5. While you are on Desktop 2, open the Photos app. Having just one application on the desktop makes working with that application a little easier.

6. Select the Task View button again. You can see, on the Desktop 2 tile, the Photos app.

7. Move the pointer or your finger onto the Desktop 2 tile, and when the Close button appears, click or tap the Close button to close Desktop 2. The Photos app that you opened on Desktop 2 now appears on Desktop 1, the only open desktop. When you close a desktop, all its open applications move to the desktop that is still open.

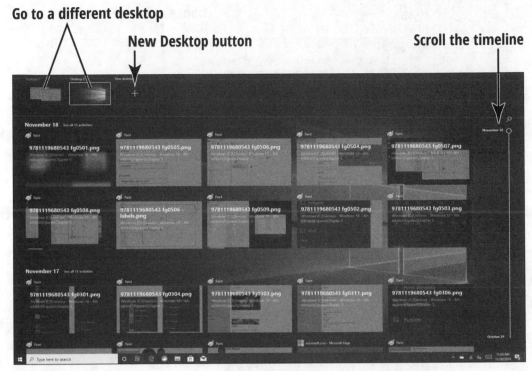

Go to a different desktop

New Desktop button

Scroll the timeline

FIGURE 5-10

Choose a Desktop Background

1. Select the Windows button to open the Start menu. Then, on the Start menu, choose Settings to open the Settings window.

2. Select Personalization. Then, in the Personalization window, select Background (if it isn't already selected). The Background screen, shown in **Figure 5-11,** is the place to go to choose a background for the Windows desktop.

TIP

You can use the Personalization window to customize many aspects of the desktop. The more time you spend on the desktop, the more worthwhile this personalization may be.

3. In the Personalization window, select Picture on the Background menu (see **Figure 5-11**).

Choose a picture

Background

Background
Picture

Choose your picture

Browse

Choose a fit
Fill

Background

Background
Solid color

Choose your background color

＋ Custom color

Choose a color

FIGURE 5-11

4. Select any photo to make that photo the desktop background. The background changes immediately. To see the entire desktop, minimize the Settings window. Restore the Settings window by selecting its icon in the taskbar or by repeating the preceding steps.

To use a photo of your own as the desktop background, select the Browse button and choose a photo in the Open dialog box.

TIP

5. On the Background menu, choose Solid Color to experiment with making a solid color the desktop background. After you choose Solid Color, a color palette appears in the Personalization screen (see **Figure 5-11**). Select a color in the color palette. The background changes immediately. What do you think of having a color background? You can minimize the Settings window to get a good look at your new desktop background.

6. Choose the background you like best — a picture or a color — on the Personalization screen and then close the Settings window.

Pin Icons to the Taskbar

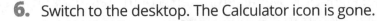

1. On the Start screen, scroll to the Calculator tile, as shown in **Figure 5-12.**

2. Use one of these methods to display the shortcut menu on the Calculator tile:

   - **Mouse:** Right-click the Calculator tile.

   - **Touchscreen:** Swipe the Calculator tile down or up slightly.

3. Select More on the shortcut menu. A submenu with more options appears (see **Figure 5-12**).

4. Select Pin to Taskbar on the submenu. Doing so places the icon for Calculator in the desktop taskbar for easy access. The Calculator icon appears in the taskbar, as shown in **Figure 5-13.**

TIP

Press ⊞+D to go directly to the desktop at any time.

5. Repeat Steps 1 and 3 and then select Unpin from Taskbar.

TIP

A fast way to remove an icon from the taskbar is to right-click it and choose Unpin from Taskbar on the shortcut menu.

6. Switch to the desktop. The Calculator icon is gone.

Pinned icons have a killer feature: *jumplists,* which are short menus of tasks and documents specific to the pinned app. To see the jumplist of a pinned app, right-click its icon in the taskbar or tap and hold on the icon until a small box appears. Try that with the File Explorer icon in the taskbar. Not all desktop apps have jumplists.

TIP

Place an application on the taskbar

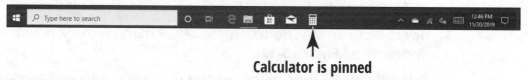

FIGURE 5-12

FIGURE 5-13

Calculator is pinned

Stop Apps with the Task Manager

1. On the desktop, select Task Manager from the taskbar context menu (shown in **Figure 5-14**) using one of these methods:

- **Mouse:** Right-click over an empty area of the taskbar and select Task Manager from the context menu.

- **Touchscreen:** Tap and hold an empty area of the taskbar until a small box appears; then release. Select Task Manager from the context menu.

- **Keyboard:** Press Ctrl+Shift+Esc to display the Task Manager directly.

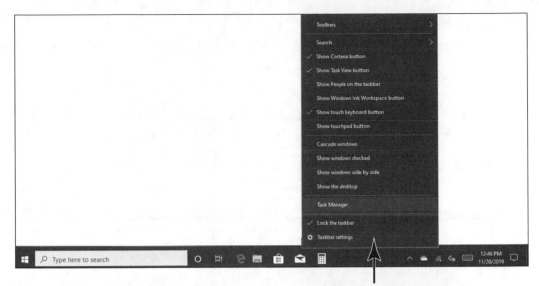

Taskbar context menu

FIGURE 5-14

2. The Task Manager lists any running apps — both desktop apps and Windows 10 apps. Select an app, also referred to as a *task*. Note that the End Task button is now available, as shown in **Figure 5-15, left.** You don't have to end this task, but you could. Any of the tasks in the Task Manager window can be ended without consequences.

TIP

Be careful about ending an app used to create something (for example, a word-processing app) because you could lose data you haven't saved before ending the task. Use the Task Manager to end tasks that you can't end otherwise, such as a frozen or locked app or one that seems to slow down everything.

3. Select the More Details option. The Task Manager expands and displays detailed information about every process running on the computer (refer to **Figure 5-15, right**). There's more to Task Manager, although you may not need all its capabilities. Select Fewer Details to return to the simpler version.

4. Close the Task Manager.

Select a task

FIGURE 5-15

2

Windows 10 and the Web

IN THIS PART . . .

Explore the Internet.

Send and receive email.

Test-drive some valuable apps.

Chapter **6**

Finding What You Need on the Web

The World Wide Web — or, simply, the web — provides quick access to information and entertainment worldwide. One part library, one part marketplace, and one part soapbox, the web makes everything equidistant. From down the block to halfway around the world — even out into space — everything is a few clicks or taps away. News, shopping, and the electronic equivalent of the town square await you.

You explore the web using a *web browser,* a program designed to make browsing the web easy, enjoyable, and safe. In this chapter, I show how you can use the Edge browser to step beyond your computer into the global village.

You browse *web pages,* which are published by governments, businesses, and individuals — anyone can create web pages. Each web page may consist of a few words or thousands of words and pictures. A web page is part of a larger collection called a *website,* which consists of a group of related web pages published on a topic by an organization or individual. Companies and individuals create websites to organize their related pages.

Pages and sites on the web have some common characteristics:

> **Unique addresses,** which are formally called *URLs* (URL stands for Uniform Resource Locator, in case you're ever on *Jeopardy!*).

> **Connecting links** that move you from page to page when you select them. These *links* (also called *hypertext links* or *hyperlinks*) often appear underlined and blue. Pictures and other graphic images can also be links to other pages. You can tell when a picture or image is a link by moving the pointer over it. The pointer changes from an arrow to a hand when it is over a hyperlink picture or image. Exploring the web using links is easier than typing URLs.

In this chapter, you use Edge to browse the web. To get the most out of browsing, you juggle multiple sites simultaneously and find out how to bookmark your favorite websites. You also find out how to search for almost anything and make use of some nice features in Edge. Finally, this chapter shows how to view web pages without seeing pesky advertisements.

TIP

Edge is by no means the only browser. Microsoft invented Edge to coincide with the release of Windows 10. You are hereby encouraged to test-drive other, more established browsers, namely Mozilla Firefox (www.mozilla.org) and Chrome (www.google.com/chrome/browser).

TIP

Edge is a relatively new invention. For many years, Windows came bundled with a browser called Internet Explorer. Internet Explorer may well be installed on your computer, but I don't recommend using it. It's difficult to use, and Microsoft doesn't support it anymore.

Browse the Web with Edge

1. Open Edge by selecting its tile on the Start screen or its icon on the taskbar. Edge opens to the *start page,* as shown in **Figure 6-1.** This page presents websites and news stories that Microsoft thinks are of interest to you based on your browsing history. If you haven't used Edge yet or haven't used it very often, you don't have a browsing history to speak of, and the websites and news stories you see here probably look quite tepid. (Later in this chapter, "Explore Edge Features" explains how to choose what web pages you see when you start Edge.)

TIP

When you start Edge, you may see an error message if you're not connected to the Internet. If so, see Chapter 4 for information on connecting. See "Bookmark and Revisit Your Favorite Websites," later in this chapter, for instructions about choosing a home page.

Address bar

FIGURE 6-1

2. Note the *address bar* at the top of the Edge screen (refer to **Figure 6-1**). In the address bar, type `www.dummies.com`. As you type, search suggestions appear in a drop-down menu. Either select `www.dummies.com` in the search suggestions or press Enter. The web page for the Dummies Press appears, as shown in **Figure 6-2.**

If you have trouble finding the address bar, try clicking with the mouse or tapping with your finger near the top of the screen, to the right of the four buttons (Back, Forward, Refresh, and Home). This will make the address bar appear.

3. Select a link on the page with a click or a tap. Where are the links? Just about everywhere. When you move the pointer over a link, it changes from an arrow to a hand — that's how you can tell where the links are.

4. Select the Back button (or press Alt+left arrow) to return to the preceding page. This button (an arrow) is located in the upper-left corner of the screen (refer to **Figure 6-2**). Select the Back button to backtrack and revisit pages.

5. Select the Forward button (or press Alt+right arrow) to move forward to the page you visited in Step 3. The Forward button is next to the Back button (refer to **Figure 6-2**). Edge remembers the pages you visit to make it easy to go forward and back.

To zoom in and make a web page look bigger, press Ctrl+plus sign. To zoom out, press Ctrl+minus sign.

6. Select the Add to Favorites or Reading List button on the right side of the screen (or press Ctrl+D). After you select this button, a Add to Favorites panel appears, as shown in **Figure 6-3.** Select the Add button to add Dummies.com to your Favorites list. Later in this chapter, "Bookmark and Revisit Your Favorite Websites" explains how to go to your favorite websites by selecting sites on the Favorites list.

You can change the text in the Add to Favorites panel before you select the Add button. However, there's usually no need to change the text unless it's overly long or unclear.

Browsing the web consists of entering addresses, following links, going forward and back, and revisiting your favorite websites. Relatively simple activities can absorb hours.

7. Keep Edge open if you want to go on to the next topic in this chapter.

Back button

Forward button

Add to Favorites or Reading List button

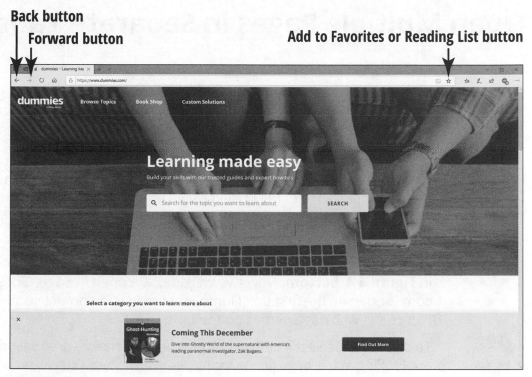

FIGURE 6-2

☆ Favorites   ≡ Reading list

Name

dummies - Learning Made Easy

Save in

Favorites ⌄

Add   Cancel

FIGURE 6-3

Open Multiple Pages in Separate Tabs

1. Open Edge if it isn't already open.

2. Go to the Google website at www.google.com. You can get there by typing www.google.com in the address bar and pressing Enter.

3. Select the New Tab button (or press Ctrl+T). This button is located to the right of the rightmost tab, as shown in **Figure 6-4, top.** A new web page appears, as shown in **Figure 6-4, middle.** What's more, a new tab (not coincidentally called New Tab) appears at the top of the screen.

4. On the new tab, enter www.dummies.com in the address bar and press Enter. You open the Dummies website on the second tab, as shown in **Figure 6-4, bottom.** Now two websites are open in Edge. Google.com is open on the first tab; Dummies.com is open on the second. Notice the web page names on the tabs.

   > **TIP** To close a tab, select its Close button (the X) or make sure that you are looking at the page you want to close and press Ctrl+W.

5. Select the first tab, the one with the name Google. You return to the Google website.

   Browsing in multiple tabs allows you to keep one page open while visiting another, perhaps to compare information or to follow a different thought.

   > **TIP** The keyboard shortcut for switching between tabs is Ctrl+Tab.

6. Select the Show Tab Previews button. This button is located to the right of the New Tab button (refer to **Figure 6-4, top**). Selecting the New Tab Previews button displays thumbnail images of websites that are open so that you can tell which website is which. You can click a thumbnail image of a website to go to a website. Select the Hide Tab Previews button to close the thumbnail images (the button is where the Show Tab Previews button used to be).

7. Select the Close button (the X) on the Dummies.com tab to close that particular tab. Close tabs when you want to reduce clutter and simplify switching among open tabs.

Show Tab Previews button

New tab button

New tab   **Switch between tabs**

FIGURE 6-4

The keyboard shortcut for closing the current tab is Ctrl+W. (*W?* Long story.)

TIP

Search for Anything

1. With Edge open, go to the address bar and type **travel.** A drop-down list of search terms with the word *travel* appears as Edge attempts to guess what you're searching for. (Ignore this list for this exercise,

but take advantage of it later.) Select Bing Search on the right side of the search term list to open the Bing website.

TIP

You can search the Internet from the Start screen without opening Edge. Type a search term in the Search box. The Search panel lists items pertaining to the search term you entered, including ideas for web searches. Select a web-related item to search with Edge.

2. A search results page appears, as shown in **Figure 6-5.** The results come from www.bing.com, which is the default search engine for Edge. A *search engine* is simply a website that provides links to web pages that match your search. (That definition, however, ignores the complex process going on behind the scenes.)

3. Scroll down the page of search results. Select any link you want to follow. If you get to the bottom of the page, select the Next button to see more search results.

TIP

Some of the "search results" are advertisements. In Bing searches, the results at the top of the page and the right side of the page are paid for. Be careful of these advertisements, which are designed to sell you something, not to provide information. If you prefer not to see advertisements on web pages, see "Block Ads on Web Pages," later in this chapter.

4. Return to the previous screen by selecting the Back button (or pressing Alt+left arrow).

5. Select the address bar and type **travel new mexico** (no capitals needed). As you type, potential matches for your terms appear in the drop-down list. If you see an item matching the search you want, select it in the list. Otherwise, press Enter.

TIP

Different search engines turn up different results. Other search engines include Google (www.google.com) and Yahoo! (www.yahoo.com). To use one of these search engines when exploring the web, enter its address in the address bar.

6. Note the tabs at the top of the Bing page, below the Search box. The first tab is All, which contains the results you see by default. Additional tabs vary with the search. Select each of the tabs, which may include any of the following:

- **Images** displays pictures matching your terms.

- **Videos** displays clips and snippets related to your search terms.

- **Maps** will help you get there.

- **News** displays search results from recent news, instead of all the results of the broader web.

- **Shopping** directs you where to shop for items that match your search term.

7. Leave Edge open if you want to move on to the next topic.

Search results (and advertisements)

FIGURE 6-5

Bookmark and Revisit Your Favorite Websites

1. Open Edge, if it isn't already open, and go to your favorite website on the Internet (or if you don't have a personal favorite, go to mine: `www.google.com/advanced_search`). If you've spent any time on the Internet, you soon find websites that you want to visit again and

again. Rather than memorize the addresses of these websites, you can add them to your Favorites list to make revisiting them quite easy.

2. Select the Add to Favorites or Reading List button (located on the right side of the address bar; it's shaped like a star). The Add to Favorites panel opens, as shown in **Figure 6-6.** Use this panel to describe the websites you want to revisit, and store their names in the Favorites panel (you'll take a look at the Favorites panel in Step 4).

FIGURE 6-6

3. Before selecting the Add button to add your favorite website to the Favorites list, consider doing the following:

   - Enter a shorter, more concise, more descriptive name in the Name text box.

   - Open the Save In menu and select a folder name to store the website in a folder. (Step 8 explains how to create folders of your own.)

4. To verify that the website you are currently visiting has been added to the Favorites list, select the Favorites button (or press Ctrl+I). The Favorites panel opens, as shown in **Figure 6-7**. Look for your website in the Favorites panel.

Favorites button

Settings button

FIGURE 6-7

5. Select the Back button to go to the website you visited previously. This button is located in the upper-left corner of the screen. Next, select the Favorites button (or press Ctrl+I) and, in the list of bookmarked websites, select the website you bookmarked in Step 3 (see **Figure 6-7**). Your favorite website opens on the screen.

TIP Don't hesitate to bookmark a website that you expect to revisit. Unless you bookmark it and add it to your Favorites list, you might not be able to find it again.

TIP To remove a website from the Favorites list, display the Favorites list, move your finger or the pointer over the website's name, display the context menu, and select Delete.

6. You can make the Favorites bar appear below the address bar, as shown in **Figure 6-8.** Merely by clicking or tapping a website name on the Favorites bar, you can go straight to a favorite website without having to open the Favorites panel. To display the Favorites bar, open the Favorites panel and select the Settings button (refer to **Figure 6-7**). In the Settings panel, choose Show the Favorites Bar (refer to **Figure 6-8**). Any website you really, really like is a candidate for the Favorites bar.

Favorites bar

Choose Show the Favorites Bar

FIGURE 6-8

7. Click anywhere onscreen except in the Favorites panel to close the Favorites panel. Then select the Favorites button to open the Favorites panel (refer to **Figure 6-7**). From here, you can manage websites that you have deemed your favorites:

- **Reorder the websites and folders:** Drag a website or folder up or down in the Favorites panel until it lands in the right place.

- **Remove a website (or folder):** Display the folder or website's context menu (right-click or touch it with your finger). Then choose Delete.

- **Create a folder:** Display the context menu by right-clicking or touching a part of the panel. Then choose Create New Folder on the context menu, scroll to the bottom of the Favorites panel, and type the folder's name.

- **Rename a website (or folder):** Display the context menu, choose Rename, and enter a new name.

TIP

Folders can be a big help in organizing and finding bookmarks in the Favorites panel. If you're the type who likes to bookmark websites, give some thought to creating folders to store your bookmarks.

8. Leave Edge open if you want to move on to the next topic.

Explore Edge Features

1. Go to your absolute favorite web page so that you can pin this web page to the Start screen. Select the Settings and More button (it's located in the upper-right corner of the screen). Then, on the drop-down menu, choose More Tools and choose Pin to This Page to Start on the submenu. Select Yes in the confirmation dialog box that asks whether you really want to pin this web page to the Start menu.

2. Close Edge and then go to the Start screen and select your favorite web page's tile. By selecting this tile, you do two things at one time — you start Edge and open it to your favorite website. Isn't that convenient?

3. Select the Favorites button, and on the left side of the panel, select History. As shown in **Figure 6-9,** the History panel opens. This panel offers the means to backtrack to websites you visited in the past hour, the past day, or the previous week.

4. Scroll to the bottom of the History panel to delve into ancient history and see websites you visited some time ago. Select a website to open it in Edge.

TIP

To erase your browsing history and remove all web page names from the History panel, select the Clear History link (shown in **Figure 6-9**).

Select History   **Clear history**

History   Clear history

ↇ Earlier today - 11/24

G Google Advanced Search   5:03 PM
   google.com/advanced_search

▶ YouTube   4:39 PM
   youtube.com

▶ dodgers score - Bing   4:12 PM
   bing.com/search?q=dodgers+score

y! Los Angeles Dodgers News, Scores, ≥ 4:03 PM
    sports.yahoo.com/mlb/teams/lad

▶ travel new mexico - Bing   3:13 PM
   bing.com/search?q=travel+new+me

▶ travel new mexico - Bing - Shopping 3:12 PM
   bing.com/shop?q=travel+new+mexi

▶ travel new mexico - Bing   3:10 PM
   bing.com/search?q=travel+new+me

▶ travelers - Bing   3:10 PM
   bing.com/search?q=travelers&form=

▶ travel - Bing   3:02 PM
   bing.com/search?q=travel&form=WI

▶ travel - Bing   3:02 PM
   bing.com/search?q=travel&form=WI

▶ travel - Bing   3:01 PM

☆ Favorites
☰ Reading list
▥ Books
⏱ History
↓ Downloads

FIGURE 6-9

5. Steps 3 and 4 demonstrate how Edge keeps track of web pages you visited, but what if you resent this kind of snooping? You can browse the web without letting Edge keep a historical record of the websites you visited. To browse in private, select the Settings and More button (it shows three dots and is located in the upper-right corner of the screen) and choose New InPrivate Window in the drop-down menu. Edge opens a second, "InPrivate" window, as shown in **Figure 6-10.**

Websites you visit privately are not recorded in the History panel. Close the InPrivate window for now (or browse a while and then close it).

You can tell when you're browsing privately because the word *InPrivate* appears in the upper-left corner of the Edge window (see **Figure 6-10**).

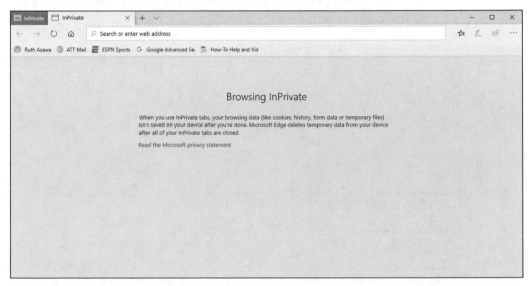

FIGURE 6-10

6. When you start Edge, you see the start page, which offers websites and news stories that Microsoft thinks you will like (refer to **Figure 6-1**). You can, however, decide for yourself what you want to see when Edge starts. Select the Favorites button, select Favorites on the left side of to the Favorites tab (if necessary), and select the Settings button. The Settings panel opens, as shown in **Figure 6-11.** Under Open Microsoft Edge With, tell Edge what you want to see first thing:

   • **Start page:** Contains websites and news stories that Microsoft thinks you will like based on your browsing history (refer to **Figure 6-1**).

   • **New tab page:** You see the Where to Next? page with an address bar and links to popular websites.

- **Previous pages:** You see web pages that you were reviewing the last time you closed Edge.

- **A specific page or pages:** After you choose this option, enter the address of the web page you want to see and select the Save button. You can enter more than one web page to open more than one when you start Edge.

7. Close Edge or keep reading if you're inclined to find out how to turn off the ads on web pages.

General   ⊸

Customize

Choose a theme

Light   ∨

Open Microsoft Edge with

Start page   ∨

Open new tabs with

"Top sites" and suggested content   ∨

Transfer favorites and other info

Import or export

Show the favorites bar

⬤ On

Show the home button

⬤ On

Set your home page

Start page   ∨

Show sites I frequently visit in "Top sites"

⬤ On

FIGURE 6-11

Block Ads on Web Pages

1. As you soon find out if you spend any time on the web, web pages are full of cumbersome advertisements. They often get in the way. How would you like to strip the ads from the web pages you visit? You can do that by installing an app from the Microsoft Store called

Adblock Plus. Chapter 9 explains how to install an app from the Microsoft Store. Close Edge, go to the Microsoft Store, and install Adblock Plus now (and visit Chapter 9, if necessary). Installing takes only half a minute. I'll wait for you here.

2. The first time you open Edge after Adblock Plus is installed, you see the message screen shown in **Figure 6-12.** Select the Turn It On button. Then go to a web page of your choice.

(ABP) You have a new extension

To start using Adblock Plus, turn it on. This extension is allowed to:

- See the websites you visit
- Read and change content on websites you visit
- Read and change anything you send or receive from websites
- Store personal browsing data on your device

[Turn it on]   [Keep it off]

FIGURE 6-12

3. **Figure 6-13** shows the same web page before and after Adblock Plus was installed. Notice the large ad at the top of the first Edge screen. This ad is absent from the same screen on the bottom of the figure. After you install Adblock Plus, the Adblock Plus button (with the letters ABP) appears in the upper-right corner of the screen (refer to **Figure 6-13**). A number next to the button tells you how many ads were blocked on the web page you're visiting.

4. Click the ABP button. You see the drop-down menu shown in **Figure 6-14, left.** It also tells you how many ads were blocked. Occasionally you run into a web page that can't be viewed when ads are blocked. In cases like that, you can turn off Adblock Plus. To do so, click the APB button, drag the slider on the drop-down menu to the left, and select the Refresh button (refer to **Figure 6-14, right**).

5. Click or tap anywhere on the web page to close the Adblock Plus drop-down menu.

Advertisement   **Adblock Plus (APB) button**

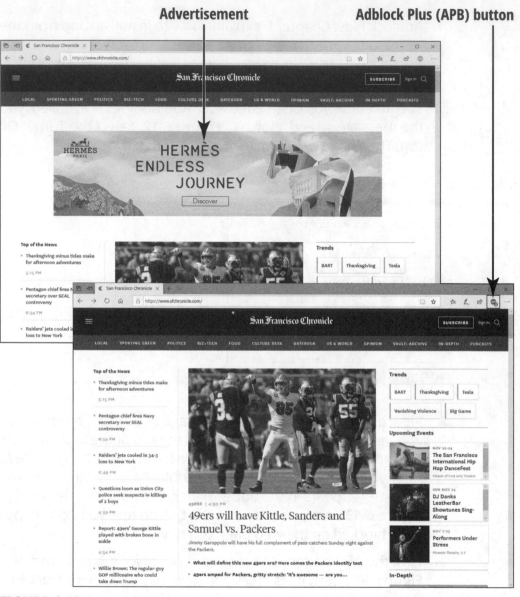

FIGURE 6-13

Drag the slider

Block ads on:
sfchronicle.com

Number of items blocked

5   on this page

2,128   in total

⊘   Block element

Block ads on:
sfchronicle.com

Click **Refresh** for the changes to take effect.

Refresh

Select Refresh

FIGURE 6-14

Chapter **7**

Emailing Family and Friends

E very day, billions of email messages circle the globe, conveying greetings, news, jokes, even condolences.

Email also provides a way to send and receive *attachments,* such as documents or photos. Who needs faxes or postcards?

The Mail app gives you access to email using your Microsoft Account. Your Microsoft Account can be associated with an email address from any email service provider, including Microsoft's own Hotmail (www. hotmail.com), Live (www.live.com), Outlook (www.outlook.com), or Xbox (www.xbox.com). You can also use email services such as Yahoo! (www.yahoo.com) and Gmail (www.gmail.com) without having a Microsoft Account. However, you have to access non–Microsoft Account email using a web browser or an app other than Microsoft's Mail app. See Chapter 6 for information on browsing the web.

In this chapter, you use the Mail app for email. You compose, format, and send email, files, and pictures. You also discover how to respond to incoming email.

TIP

If you don't have a physical keyboard, see Chapter 1 for information on using the virtual keyboard.

Use the Mail App

1. For email on Windows 10, select the Mail tile on the Start screen or the Mail icon on the taskbar. The Mail app opens. If you're currently signed in to your Microsoft Account, the Mail app knows your email address. (You gave it to Microsoft when you created the account.) This address is listed on the Mail screen, and you're ready to go. If you're not currently signed in using a Microsoft Account, enter your email address and password on the Sign In screen that appears and then select Sign In. (See Chapter 4 for information on creating a Microsoft Account.)

TIP

The first time you use the Mail app, you are invited to "add an account." In other words, Windows 10 offers its help linking an email account you have to the Mail app. Select the Add Account button and follow the onscreen instructions for making an email account available to the Mail app. See "Add an Email Account to Mail," later in this chapter, for more information.

2. When you start the Mail app, you land in the Inbox folder. If you haven't used your Microsoft Account for email, you probably don't have any messages in your Inbox folder. Who would have written you already? You may, however, see a message or two from Microsoft.

3. On the Inbox screen, select the Expand/Collapse button, as shown in **Figure 7-1.** The Folders panel expands, and you can see the names of all your folders in the Folders panel. In the Mail app, email is kept in folders.

TIP

The number beside each folder name tells you how many unread email messages are in each folder.

Select the Expand/Collapse button to expand the Folders panel

Conduct a search

New Mail button

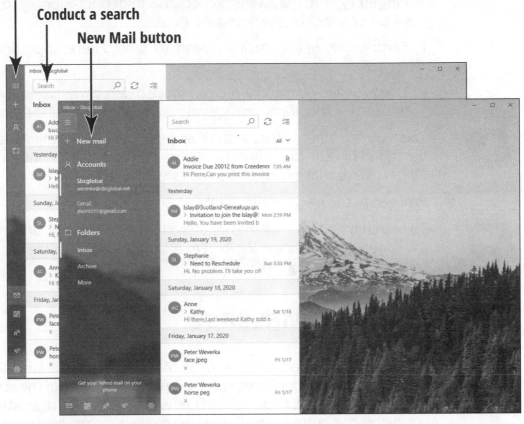

FIGURE 7-1

4. Select any of the following folders in the Folders panel and then select the Expand/Collapse button to return to the Mail panel (you have to select More in the Folders panel to see some of these folders):

- **Inbox:** Email you have received but not moved elsewhere appears here, including both read and unread email.

- **Archive:** The Mail app provides this folder for email that you want to keep on hand for archival purposes.

- **Drafts:** As you compose email (see next section), you can save your message as a draft until you are ready to send it.

- **Junk:** Messages are moved here — either automatically or by you — instead of the Inbox, if they are suspected of being, well, *junk*. The more common term for unwanted email is *spam*. (It's a long story.) You may want to check this folder occasionally to see whether a message was misfiled here.

- **Sent:** Copies of the email you send are stored here, appropriately enough.

- **Trash:** Self-explanatory? You can move deleted messages out of the Trash folder if you change your mind about deleting them.

You may see other folders in the Folders panel besides the folders described here. If you linked the Mail app to an email account with other folders, those folders are also listed in the Folders panel.

5. Proceed to the next section, "Write an Email Message."

To search for stray email messages, go to the Search box, and enter the content you're searching for. For example, enter a subject, sender, or something in the message.

Write an Email Message

1. To compose an email message in the Mail app, select the New Mail button (it looks like a plus sign) in the upper-left corner of the screen (refer to **Figure 7-1**). (It doesn't matter which folder you're in when you select this button.) The Compose screen appears, as shown in **Figure 7-2.**

2. In the To box, type an email address. If the Mail app recognizes the address because you've sent email to or received email from the person to whom you're addressing your message, a pop-up box appears so that you can select the person's address without having to type it. Press the Tab key, touch the screen, or use the mouse to move to the next option.

To send email to more than one person at one time, select the Cc & Bcc button (located to the right of the address line). Then type a recipient's address in the Cc box (and the Bcc box as well, if you want to send a blind copy without revealing you've done so). (Once upon a time, *CC* stood for *carbon copy,* and then it became *courtesy copy.*) Technically, it makes no difference whether you use additional To addresses or the CC.

3. Enter a few words in the Subject box describing your message's content or purpose.

4. Select below the Subject line. Type your message. Avoid all caps; purists consider caps to be SHOUTING! No need to press Enter as you approach the end of the line — this isn't a typewriter.

TIP

Some people start a message with a salutation, such as *Hi Peter*, but many people do not. Some people sign email using their initials. Email can be as formal or casual as you choose to make it.

Words underlined with a red squiggle aren't recognized by Windows 10 and may be misspelled. Right-click or tap and hold to see a pop-up menu, and choose Proofing on the menu. You see a list of suggested spellings. Choose the correct spelling if it is on the list. You can also go to the Options tab and select the Spelling button there.

5. When you're ready to send the message, select the Send button (you'll find it in the upper-right corner of the Compose window; refer to **Figure 7-2**). If you decide not to send the message, select the Discard button.

TIP

Email you compose but haven't sent yet is kept in the Drafts folder. You can postpone writing a message and finish it later by going to the Drafts folder and opening your message there. To go the Drafts folder, select the Expand/Collapse button (if necessary) and then select Drafts in the All Folders panel.

6. If you select the Send button, your message is sent and you return to the folder you were in at the beginning of Step 1.

7. Repeat from Step 1 as needed.

Mail puts a signature at the bottom of email messages: "Sent from Mail for Windows 10." If you don't like this signature or want to put your own signature at the bottom of all the emails you send, select the Settings button on the bottom of the Folders panel. The Settings panel opens. Select Signature and either turn off signatures or enter a signature of your own.

Enter an email address   **Send the message**

Format   Insert   Draw   Options   🗑 Discard   ➤ Send

B *I* U̲ ∨ ☰ ☰ ∨   Heading 1 ∨   ↺ Undo   ↻ Redo

From: weverka@sbcglobal.net

To: Anne;   👤 Cc & Bcc

The Cat

Hello Anne:

Did you feed the cat?

--Peter

Sent from Mail for Windows 10

FIGURE 7-2

Format Email

1. If you want to add bold, italics, or other formats to email, select the text you want to fancy up in the Compose window, as shown in **Figure 7-3.** If no text is selected, your formatting will apply to the word in which the *cursor* (the blinking vertical line in the content) is located.

   - **Mouse:** Click and drag the mouse pointer over the text you want to select.

   - **Touchscreen:** Tap and drag over the text you want to select.

   - **Keyboard:** With the cursor at the beginning of the text you want to select, hold down the Shift key as you press the right or down arrow to select text. Release the Shift key only after you have completed your selection.

Format the text

From: weverka@sbcglobal.net

To: Anne;   Cc & Bcc

The Cat

Hello Anne:

Did you feed the cat?

--Peter

Sent from Mail for Windows 10

Select the text

FIGURE 7-3

To apply formatting to one word, double-click or double-tap that word to select it and display the app bar in one step.

The keyboard shortcut to select all text is Ctrl+A. No mouse or touch-screen method is quite so complete.

2. Using the commands on the Format tab, select from the following formatting options:

- **Bold:** Bold is used for emphasis to make text stand out.

- **Italic:** Although italic can also be used for emphasis, it may be harder to read than normal or bold text.

- **Underline:** Because links are usually underlined automatically, you may want to avoid underlining text that isn't a link.

- **Bulleted list:** Select the Bullets button and enter items for the list. As you enter items, Mail attaches a bullet point to the start of each line.

- **Numbered list:** Select the Numbering button and type the list. As you type, Mail assigns a number to each line.

- **Styles:** Choose a style from the drop-down menu. A style applies many formats simultaneously. Heading 1, for example, enlarges the text and turns it blue.

See Chapter 1 for information on using the virtual keyboard's emoticons.

To create a hyperlink, go to the Insert tab and select the Link button. Then enter the address destination of the hyperlink in the address bar that appears. See Chapter 6 for more information about hyperlinks.

3. When you finish formatting the text, select the Send button.

Send Files and Pictures

1. To send a file or picture with your email message, go to the Insert tab. As shown in **Figure 7-4,** the Insert tab offers tools for sending files and pictures.

2. Select the Files button to send a file. The Open dialog box appears. Locate and select the file you want to send and then select the Open button in the dialog box. You can send more than one file with an email message. In the Compose window, files you want to send appear as thumbnails under the heading "Attachments" (see **Figure 7-4**). Click the X button on a file if you change your mind about sending it.

3. To send a picture with an email message, place the cursor where you want the picture to be. Then select the Pictures button on the Insert tab. The Open dialog box appears. Select the picture and then click or tap the Insert button.

You can format pictures before sending them. Click or tap a picture to select it in the Compose window. The Picture tab appears. Using the tools on this tab, you can rotate, crop, and resize pictures.

FIGURE 7-4

4. When you have finished attaching your files and pictures, select the Send button to send them on their merry way.

TIP

Chapter 10 explains how you can use the Photos app to send photos to others.

Read and Respond to Incoming Email

1. On the Start screen, select the Mail tile. The Mail app opens to the Inbox folder.

2. Select a message under the Inbox heading. The content of the message appears to the right, as shown in **Figure 7-5.**

TIP

In email terminology, bouncing messages back and forth with someone about the same subject is called a *conversation*. When you select an email message that is part of a conversation, the other messages in the conversation appear as well so that you can select and reread them (refer to **Figure 7-5**).

3. After you read the message, you can respond to or forward it if you want. Select the Reply or Reply All button to reply; select the Forward button to forward the message. Selecting any of these buttons starts a new message (refer to **Figure 7-2**) that includes the text of the original message. The subject line is automatically *RE: [the original subject]* (in the case of replies) or *FW: [the original subject]* (in the case of forwarded messages). Complete your message and select the Send button.

TIP

Reply All sends your response to all the other recipients, if a message is addressed to more than one person. The Reply option sends your response only to the sender. Select Forward to send the selected message to someone else. You can add your own text or remove portions of the forwarded message in the process.

TIP

See the sections "Write an Email Message" and "Format Email," earlier in this chapter, for more information on composing an email message.

4. Select any message in the Inbox category. Note the following options for managing messages (to take advantage of some of these options, select the More button in the upper-right corner of the screen):

- **Delete:** Use this option to delete the message.

- **Set Flag:** Use this option to place a flag icon next to the message in the Inbox so that you remember to deal with the message later on. You can swipe right to flag a message.

- **Mark Unread/Read:** Use this option if you want the message to appear unread (marked with a horizontal blue line in the Inbox). Select the More button (the three dots on the right side of the toolbar) to see this option. Some people mark a message as unread when they want to deal with it later.

- **Move:** Use this option to move the selected email from one folder to another. To access the Move option, select the More button (refer to **Figure 7-5**). After you select Move on the More drop-down menu, select a folder in the Move To panel to move your email.

A conversation **Reply to or forward a message** **More button**

Select to read a message **Manage messages**

[Screenshot of the Mail application interface showing the Inbox with a conversation view. Visible labels include: Search, Inbox, New mail, Accounts, Sbcglobal, weverka@sbcglobal.net, Gmail, pletb@gmail.com, Folders, Inbox, Archive, More. Messages shown for Monday, January 20, 2020; Sunday, January 19, 2020; Saturday, January 18, 2020. The reading pane displays "Re: Need to Reschedule" from Stephanie. Toolbar options: Reply, Reply all, Forward, Archive, Delete, Set flag, and a dropdown menu with Mark as unread, Move, Previous, Next, Find, Save as, Print, Zoom.]

FIGURE 7-5

TIP

If you add email accounts from providers such as Gmail, you may see additional categories or options. See the section "Add an Email Account to Mail" at the end of the chapter.

Change Mail Settings

1. In Mail, display the Settings panel, shown in **Figure 7-6.** To display the Settings panel, display the Folder panel and select the Settings button (you'll find it in the lower-right corner of the Folder panel). The Settings panel appears on the right side of the Mail screen.

2. On the Accounts panel, select Manage Accounts, and then select the email account with settings that need a change. The Account Settings dialog box appears (see **Figure 7-7, left**).

3. Negotiate the Account Settings dialog box and select the Save button:

   • **Account Name:** The name of the email service provider. You can change this, if you want. I might use *Peter's email*.

- **Change Mailbox Sync Settings:** Click or tap here to open the Sync Settings dialog box (see **Figure 7-7, right**) and change how and when the Mail app collects email. Skip to Step 5 if you choose this option.

- **Delete Account:** Deletes the email account. The Mail app is no longer associated with the account after you delete it.

Settings

Manage accounts

Manage subscriptions

Personalization

Automatic replies

Focused inbox

Message list

Reading pane

Signature

Default Font

Notifications

Email security

What's new

Outlook for Android and iOS

Help

Trust Center

Feedback

About

FIGURE 7-6

4. In the Sync Settings dialog box (refer to **Figure 7-7, right**), choose settings and select the Done button:

- **Download New Content:** If you don't want email constantly streaming into your Inbox, you can change this setting to every 15 or 30 minutes, Hourly, or only when you select the Sync This View button (which is located next to the Search button).

- **Always Download Full Message and Internet Images:** Select this option if pictures aren't appearing in your incoming email messages.

- **Download Email From:** You can limit how far back to download messages to your computer. This setting isn't relevant in a new email account.

- **Sync Options:** Turn the Email setting to Off only if you don't want the Mail app to receive email from the account. Turn the other two settings, Calendar and Contacts, to Off if — for the purpose of privacy — you don't want the Mail app to retrieve information from the Calendar app or People app.

Change Sync settings

Delete the account

FIGURE 7-7

Add an Email Account to Mail

1. If you have another email address, you can add it to Mail. Adding an account has definite advantages. Instead of going hither and yon to collect your email from different accounts, you can collect all your mail in one place — the Mail app. The following steps explain how to add an existing Gmail account to Mail. In Mail, display the Settings panel (refer to **Figure 7-6**) and then select Manage Accounts.

2. In the Manage Accounts panel, select Add Account.

Many people have more than one email address. Your Internet service provider probably gave you an email account, and you may have another through work or school. However, this feature isn't for everyone.

3. In the Add an Account dialog box, select the service with which you have an email account. If your service doesn't appear here, select Other Account. If you have a Gmail address (or you just want to see what's next), select Google.

4. On the Connecting to a Service screen, enter your Gmail address, select Next, and enter your password in the appropriate box. Then select Next. Select the Back button if you don't want to continue.

5. The next screen informs you how your Gmail account will connect with the Mail app. Scroll to the bottom of this screen and select the Allow button.

6. In the dialog box that says you've added an account, select Go to Inbox.

7. Return to the Manage Accounts folder (select the Settings button and choose Manage Accounts in the Settings panel). As shown in **Figure 7-8,** the Manage Accounts panel shows you the names of your accounts. You can switch to a different account by selecting its name in the Manage Accounts panel.

See the preceding section, "Change Mail Settings," for the steps to review or change settings for your newly added account.

FIGURE 7-8

Chapter **8**

Exploring Apps for Your Daily Life

This chapter describes a handful of apps that the average Joe or Jane might use every day. It shows how to store contact information — names, email addresses, phone numbers, and the like — in the People app so that you can find this information quickly. You also use the Calendar app to keep track of birthdays, anniversaries, appointments, and other events.

This chapter delves into the Maps app, showing you how to use it to get directions and to look up hotels and restaurants when you're on the go. You see how two Windows 10 apps, Sticky Notes and Alarms & Clock, can help you complete tasks on time, and how WordPad can help you with your word processing chores.

Finally, this chapter demonstrates how to make the Lock screen indicate whether you've received email, how to chat face-to-face with family and friends over the Internet with Skype, and how to ask questions of Cortana.

Add Contacts to the People App

1. On the Start screen, select the People app.

TIP

You need a Microsoft Account to use Mail, Calendar, and People. When you sign in to one, you're signed in to all three apps. See Chapter 4 for information on creating a Microsoft Account.

2. If you haven't signed in already using your Microsoft Account, the Sign In screen appears. Enter your Microsoft Account email address or your phone number, enter your password, and then select Sign In.

3. What you see first in People depends on whether the app found contact information associated with your Microsoft Account. You may see familiar names or an invitation to connect to other services. For now, add a new contact manually. (You connect to other services later.) Display the New Contact screen by selecting the New Contact button, as shown in **Figure 8-1.**

TIP

The first time you run the People app, you are greeted with a Welcome screen. Select the Get Started button on this screen. If you manage your email through the Mail app (a subject covered in Chapter 7), you can load contact information from the Mail app into the People App. On the Let's Get Started screen, select the Ready to Go button.

4. Much of the information on the New Contact screen (shown in **Figure 8-1**) is optional. Enter the information that you want access to throughout Windows 10, not just in the People app. (For example, think about what you want to access in Mail.) You can enter any person's name and information you want, but let me suggest the following:

- **Save To:** Ultimately, you may link multiple accounts using the People app. Which account do you want this new contact associated with? For now, only one option may be available.

- **Name:** Enter the contact's full name.

- **Mobile Phone:** Select Mobile Phone and note the many categories of phone numbers — Home, Work Company, and so on — on the pop-up list.

New Contact button   Enter contact info

FIGURE 8-1

- **Personal Email:** Select Personal Email and notice the three email categories — Personal, Work, and Other — on the pop-up list. Choose a category and enter the contact's email address.

5. Note the following buttons with plus signs. Select each in turn to see the available options. Add data as you please:

   - **Email:** Add up to two more email addresses.

   - **Phone:** Add up to seven more phone numbers!

   - **Address:** Add up to three mailing addresses.

   - **Other:** Options include Job Title, Significant Other, Website, and Notes, a box for free-form notes.

6. When you're done, select Save to add this contact (or select Cancel to throw away the new contact). The added contact appears on your list of contacts. Select the person's name to see his or her contact information, as shown in **Figure 8-2.**

![Contact card for Peter showing a photo. Toolbar icons at top: pin, share, delete.]

Peter

Contact			🖉 Edit
Mobile phone			
111-222-333	📞 Call with Viber	📞 Call with Skype	...
Other email			
wev@global.net			✉ Email
Other email			
B6E@outlook.com			✉ Email
Home address			
11 Main St.			🗺 Map
Anytown, NY 02134			

See more >

FIGURE 8-2

To edit a contact's information, select his or her name, display the context menu (by right-clicking or tapping), and choose Edit. The Contact screen appears so that you can edit away.

You can pin a contact to the taskbar. Select the person's name, display the context menu (by right-clicking or tapping), and choose Pin to Taskbar.

Delete a Contact

1. Open the People app if the People app isn't already open.

2. In the Contacts list on the left side of the screen, select the name of the contact you want to delete. Especially if your list of contacts is a lengthy one, it pays to go through the list from time to time and delete the names of people you are no longer associated with.

TIP

On the People screen, enter a letter or type a name in the Search box. Entering a letter produces a drop-down list of names that start with the letter you entered. Typing a name produces a list of names. Select a name on the list to go to the name.

3. Select the Delete button, shown in **Figure 8-3.**

4. In the Delete Contact? dialog box that asks whether you really want to do it, select the Delete button (refer to **Figure 8-3**).

Delete button

People
b

Name	Email
J	
Julie	Julie@lr.com
K	
Kenyon	kbro@.com
Kyle	kloc
L	
Lasselle	
M	
Mark	ms@L.com
Max	gt@mail.com
Melissa	mel@hoo.com
Michael	ml@wiley.com
Michael	phat@mail.com

A   AT&T

Contact   ✎ Edit

Other email
ettlement@tgcginc.com   ✉ Email

See more ›

Delete contact?

AT&T will be deleted from the People app and from Sbcglobal.

| Delete | Cancel |

this contact will show up here.

Conversations

Recent conversations with this contact will show up here.

Combined contacts

Suggested

Find a contact to combine

FIGURE 8-3

Add a Birthday or Anniversary to the Calendar

1. To see the calendar and add events, open the Calendar app from the Start screen, as shown in **Figure 8-4.** You may see events and appointments from services you connected to in People or Mail.

2. On the Calendar app bar located along the top of the screen (refer to **Figure 8-4**), select each of the following formats:

- **Day:** This format displays a single day with a box for each hour. Select arrows near the top of the screen to scroll back or forward one day at a time. Scroll up and down to see more hours in the day.

- **Week:** The current week appears. Scroll or use the arrows to go from hour to hour or week to week.

TIP

  Open the drop-down menu on the Week button and choose Work Week to see the current workweek (Monday through Friday).

- **Month:** The current month appears in the classic month layout. (Depending on the size of your screen, you may have to scroll to see this format.) Today is highlighted with a different color. Use arrows near the top to move forward and back a month at a time.

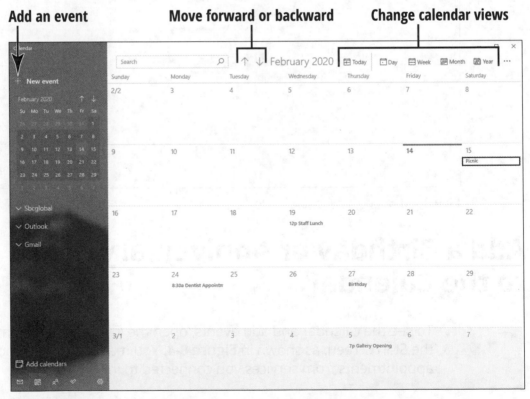

FIGURE 8-4

- **Year:** The months of the year appear. You can select a month to open a month in Month view.

TIP

Select the Today button on the Calendar app bar to go immediately to today's date on the Calendar.

3. The Calendar offers two ways to add an event, the short-but-cursory way and the slow-but-thorough way:

- **Short but cursory:** Click or tap the day on which the event is to occur (in the Month format) or the hour and date on which it is to occur (in the Day or Week formats). You see the pop-up window shown in **Figure 8-5.** With luck, this little window is all you need to describe the event. Type the event's name, and if it isn't an all-day event, deselect the All Day check box (if necessary) and use the start time and end time menus to describe when the event starts and ends. You can also type the event's location. Select the Save button when you finish describing the event (or select the More Details link to open the Details screen and go to Step 4).

- **Slow but thorough:** Select the New Event button (refer to **Figure 8-4**). The Details screen appears, as shown in **Figure 8-6.** Move on to Step 4.

Pietro - Gmail ⌄	✕
Staff Meeting	☐ All day
🕐 11:00 AM ⌄ to 12:00 PM ⌄	
📍 Room 102|	
🔄 Repeat: Never ⌄	
🔔 Remind me: 15 minutes before ⌄	
More details Save	

↑
Open the Details screen

FIGURE 8-5

4. Under Details, enter or (or change) any of the following data for the event:

- **Event Name:** Describe the event in one to three words. The description you enter will appear on your calendar.

- **Location:** If listing the location will help you get to the event on time, by all means list it. The location, like the event name, appears on the calendar.

- **Start and End:** Select the calendar icon, and on the pop-up menu that appears, choose the day on which the event begins and then the day on which it ends.

- **Hours/All Day:** If this isn't an all-day event, deselect the All Day check box, if necessary. Then use the drop-down menus to describe when the event will occur.

TIP

If the event is one that recurs, you can schedule it on a weekly, monthly, or yearly basis on the calendar. Weekly staff meetings, birthdays, and anniversaries are examples of recurring events. Select the Repeat button on the app bar along the top of the screen to schedule a recurring event. Then, using the Repeat options that appear in the Details screen, describe how often the event occurs, when it occurs, and when it will cease occurring.

- **Event Description:** Describe the event in detail if you think it's necessary. Should you wear the tux or zoot suit? The ball gown or the formal dress? This is the place to record your thoughts on the matter.

5. Optionally, use the commands on the app bar at the top of the screen to further describe the event:

- **Show As:** Choose an option on this menu if you share your calendar with someone, such as a receptionist, who may schedule you for other events. You can declare yourself free, tentative, busy, or out of the office.

- **Reminder:** How far in advance of the event do you want Calendar to display a notification? Choose None, 5 Minutes, 15 Minutes, 30 Minutes, 1 Hour, 12 Hours, 1 Day, or 1 Week.

- **Private:** Select this option (look for the lock symbol) to prevent this event from appearing on a shared or public calendar. The event remains visible on your own screen.

6. When you're done, select the Save button. (Select the Delete button if you don't want to create an event.)

7. On the calendar, your event appears on the specified date and time.

8. To edit an event, select it on the calendar. A pop-up screen appears with details about the event. Select the event's name in the pop-up screen to open the Details screen, where you can add or change any detail.

Calendar

Home   Format   Review

Save   Delete   Show as: Busy   Reminder: 15 minutes   Repeat   Zoom

Details   People

Staff Lunch   Invite someone

                                                       Sort by   Original order
Location

Start: February 19, 2020   12:00 PM   All day   Me
                                                            piet@ail.com
End: February 19, 2020   1:30 PM

Don't be late.

FIGURE 8-6

To delete an event, open it in the Details screen and select the Delete button (a trash can).

If your Microsoft Account is connected to a third-party service such as Gmail, events from that service appear on your calendar. To load third-party service information into the Calendar app, select the Settings button (in the lower-left corner of the screen) and select

Manage Accounts in the Settings panel. You see a list of accounts. Select the account, and in the Account Settings screen, select Change Mailbox Sync Settings. Then, on the Sync Settings screen, choose whether to sync the calendar on the third-party service with the calendar you see in the Calendar screen.

Search and Explore with the Maps App

1. Select the Maps app on the Start menu to open the Maps app. Use this app to locate places and to get driving or walking directions.

2. Click or tap in the Search box. A drop-down list appears. It lists items you already searched for, if you searched already. You can select an item on the list to revisit it.

3. Type **1 california st, san francisco** (you don't need to enter capital letters) in the Search box. As you type, options appear in the Search panel. Select the address you entered, not the names of businesses located at the address. As shown in **Figure 8-7,** the Maps app shows you where the address is located; it also provides a photo. As well as typing addresses in the Search box, you can enter the names of places and landmarks.

4. Select the Zoom Out button (or press Ctrl+minus sign) on the app bar in the map. Then select the Zoom In button (or press Ctrl+plus sign). The tools on the app bar can help you read the map better (refer to **Figure 8-7**).

5. Select the Directions button (refer to **Figure 8-7**), which is the button in the upper-right corner near the Search box (or press Ctrl+D). Tools appear to help you get from place to place. Click or tap in the Starting Point box (Box A), and when the drop-down menu appears, choose **1 California St,** the address you already entered. In the Destination box (Box B), enter **1501 haight st** and choose the 1501 Haight St address in San Francisco in the drop-down menu that appears.

6. Select the **Get Directions** link. As shown in **Figure 8-8,** the Maps app gives you several sets of driving directions between the two addresses and tells you how long each drive will take. Select a drive in the list to get specific instructions for driving between the two

addresses. After you select a drive, you can click or tap the Print icon to print the instructions.

Enter an address or search term

Directions button

Zoom in and out

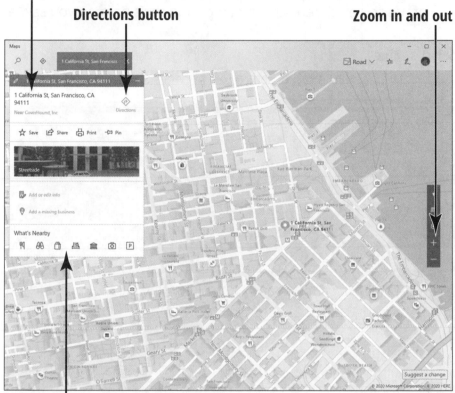

Find restaurants, hotels, and other goodies

FIGURE 8-7

7. Are you walking, not driving? In that case, select the Walking icon at the top of the Search panel to get directions for walking between the two locations. You can also select the Transit icon to get directions for getting there by public transportation.

8. Select the Search button (the magnifying glass in the upper-left corner of the screen) and then select **1501 Haight St., San Francisco** in the drop-down menu. You get a detailed look at the streets surrounding this address. Select the Restaurants icon under What's Nearby (refer to **Figure 8-7**) to see restaurants on the map. You can select the name of a restaurant to find out more about it. The What's Nearby icons also provide the means to find attractions, parking, hotels, and other goodies.

9. The Maps app keeps tabs on your travels. Select a tab along the top of the screen to retrace your steps and revisit a map you saw earlier.

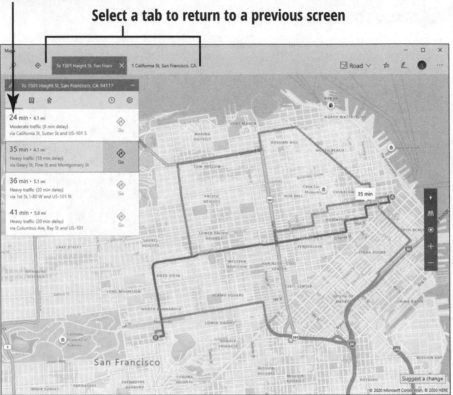

Select a route

Select a tab to return to a previous screen

FIGURE 8-8

Remind Yourself to Do Tasks with Alarms & Clock

1. Select the Alarms & Clock app on the Start menu to open the Alarms & Clock app. Use this convenient little app to remind yourself when something needs doing, find out what time it is in other parts of the world, or time an activity.

2. To make your computer remind you when a task needs completing, select Alarm (if it isn't already selected) on the app bar along the top of the screen. Then select the Add New Alarm button (the plus sign in the lower-right corner). You see the New Alarm screen, shown in **Figure 8-9, left.**

Describe the alarm   **Click arrow to set the time**

Select Save

Snooze or dismiss

FIGURE 8-9

3. Set the alarm to ring in 2 minutes. Note the time on the clock on your computer and use the scroll arrows on the screen to set the time to 2 minutes from now. To set the time, click or tap the arrows above and below the hour, minute, and AM/PM settings until you see "In 2 Minutes" on the screen.

4. Click or tap the generic name Alarm (1) and enter a descriptive name in its place. Then select the Save button.

5. In 2 minutes, the alarm goes off and a notice appears in the lower-right corner of your computer screen (refer to **Figure 8-9, right**). It tells you the task that needs doing. Select Dismiss (or Snooze if you want the alarm to go off one more time in 5 minutes or the Snooze amount you set).

6. Click or tap the Back button (in the upper-left corner of the Alarms & Clock window) to backtrack. Then select World Clock on the app bar. From the World Clock screen, you can see what time it is in different cities and find out how many hours ahead or behind they are, as shown in **Figure 8-10.** To enter a city on the world map, select the Add New Clock button and enter the city's name in the Enter a Location box.

7. Select Stopwatch on the app bar along the top of the screen. The next time you want to see how long it takes you to complete a task, go to the Stopwatch screen and select the Start button. When the task is complete, return and select Pause.

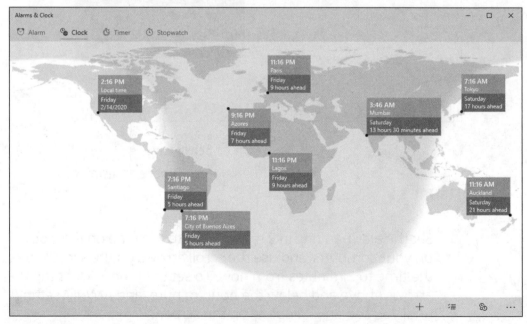

FIGURE 8-10

Write Documents with WordPad

1. Windows 10 comes with a word processing app called WordPad. Word processors are applications that you can use to write letters, reports, and other documents. WordPad isn't as sophisticated as its cousin Microsoft Word, the world's most famous word processor, but it's pretty darn good. And it doesn't cost anything. Moreover, you can open documents created in Word in WordPad. Word can read WordPad documents, too. To start WordPad, type **WordPad** in the Search box in the lower-left corner of the Windows screen and choose WordPad on the pop-up menu. WordPad opens, as shown in **Figure 8-11.**

TIP

For reasons I don't understand, WordPad isn't available on the alphabetical list of app names on the Start screen. The only way to start WordPad is to type its name in the Search box, pin WordPad to the Start menu, or pin it to the taskbar and start it from there. Chapter 5 explains pinning apps to the Start menu and taskbar.

FIGURE 8-11

2. Type a few words and then select the words by dragging over them. You can tell when words are selected because they are highlighted. After you select words, you can reformat them. Open the Font Family menu on the toolbar and choose your favorite font. Then open the Font Size menu and choose a font size. By changing fonts and font sizes, you can change the words' appearance.

3. Click or tap the Bold button (the B) on the Home tab (or press Ctrl+B). The words are boldfaced. Boldfacing, italicizing (select the Italic button), and underlining (select the Underline button) are other ways to change the appearance of words.

4. Select the Linespace button and choose an option — 1.0, 1.15, 1.5, or 2 — on the drop-down list that appears. In this way, you can change the amount of space between lines. For example, choosing 2 double-spaces the text you selected.

TIP

You can choose formatting commands *before* you start typing. The commands you choose are applied to the words you write next. It isn't necessary to write the words first and then select them to make formatting changes.

5. Drag the Zoom slider in the lower-right corner of the screen to the right (or click or tap the Zoom In button on the right side of the slider). Zooming in increases the size of text on the screen so that you can see it better. Drag the slider to the left (or click or tap the Zoom Out button) to make the text look smaller.

6. Press Ctrl+S or select the Save button (located in the upper-left corner of the screen) to save your document. You see the Save As dialog box. WordPad documents are saved in the RTF format (RTF stands for *rich text format*). As I mention earlier, Microsoft Word can read and display RTF files. Enter a name for your document and select the Save button.

TIP

Chapter 14 explains how to open, save, and otherwise manage files.

Write a Sticky Note to Yourself

1. Select Sticky Notes on the Start menu to open the Sticky Notes app. A sticky note — like the ones in **Figure 8-12** — appears on the screen. Sticky notes are the digital equivalents of the yellow stick-'em tabs that people attach to their computers and desks. Use sticky notes to remind yourself to do something or be somewhere.

FIGURE 8-12

2. Type the note. Then move the pointer over the stripe at the top of the note and drag the note to a corner of the screen.

You can change the size of a sticky note. Move the pointer over the lower-right corner of the note. When the pointer changes to double arrows, start dragging.

3. Click or tap the Add Note button (refer to **Figure 8-12**). Another sticky note appears. Write a second note and drag it to a corner of the screen.

4. Click or tap the Delete Note button on one of your notes (refer to **Figure 8-12**).

Tweak Quick Status Settings

1. Quick Status settings appear on the Lock screen to show you what's what. To change these settings, click ⊞ to open the Start screen and select Settings. On the Settings screen, select Personalization. On the Personalization screen, select Lock Screen.

   See Chapter 3 for information about the Lock Screen settings.

2. Scroll to the bottom of the Lock Screen settings to the Choose Which Apps Show Quick Status item, as shown in **Figure 8-13.**

3. Some apps can display quick status information on the Lock screen. For example, Mail displays the number of unread messages in the Mail app. To add an app to the Lock screen, select one of the plus signs and choose an app name on the pop-up menu.

TIP

FIGURE 8-13

4. To change one of the current apps, select its icon and then choose a different app on the pop-up menu.

5. To remove an app from the Lock screen, select it and choose None on the pop-up menu.

6. Return to the Start screen.

Chat Face-to-Face with Skype

1. On the Start screen, select the Skype app. You can use this app to video chat with others. To use Skype, your computer must have audio and video capability. You can also use Skype if a webcam is connected to your computer.

   TIP
   You need to sign in to your Microsoft Account before you use Skype. See Chapter 4 for information about creating a Microsoft Account.

   TIP
   The easiest way to make calls through Skype is to enter the names of the people you want to call on your Contacts list in the People app. See "Add Contacts to the People App," earlier in this chapter.

2. The first time you use the Skype app, the screen asks whether it can access your camera, microphone, and Contacts. Select Yes on all counts.

3. The Skype screen lists the names of people on your Contacts list (from the People app) and people you have called before using Skype. You can select one of these people to call them now. If the person you want to call isn't listed, enter his or her name in the Search Skype box and select the Search button (which looks like a magnifying glass). The Skype directory opens, as shown in **Figure 8-14.** Scroll to find the person you want to call, using the person's photo ID and geographical information as your guide.

4. When you see the name of the person you want to call, select the name. Then, on the call screen, select the Video Call button (refer to **Figure 8-14**). You hear a ring tone as the call is made, and you see the person's face if he or she answers, as shown in **Figure 8-15.** Your face appears in the lower-right corner of the screen so that you can see what your face looks like to the caller, (You can drag this screen from place to place.) Start talking. Smile. Trade the latest news. Have a ball.

Search **Select a name**   **Start the call**

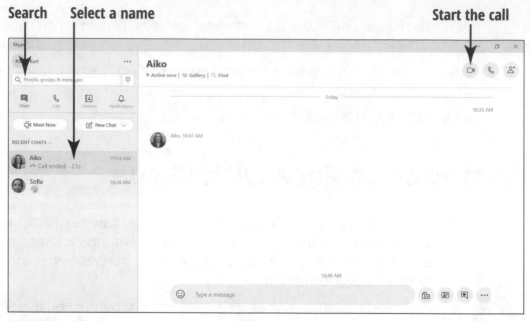

FIGURE 8-14

Open Conversation button

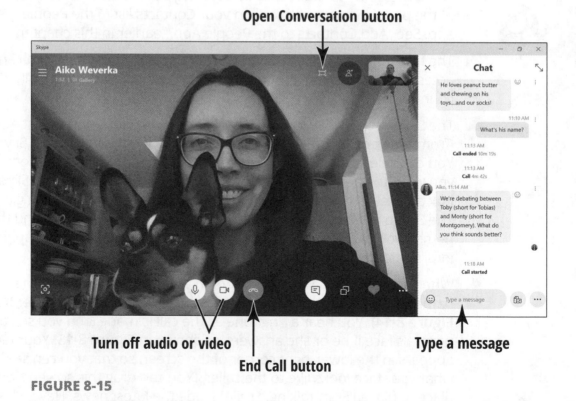

Turn off audio or video   **Type a message**

End Call button

FIGURE 8-15

TIP

Select the Video and Microphone buttons when you need a little privacy (refer to **Figure 8-15**). Select the Video button to turn off your video (the other caller can't see you); select the Microphone button to turn off your audio (the other caller can't hear you).

TIP

Select the Open Conversation button (in the upper-right corner of the screen) to send an instant message to the other caller (refer to **Figure 8-15**). The message panel appears. In the bottom of the message panel (refer to **Figure 8-15**), type your message and press Enter. Sending text messages is a useful way to communicate when you have technical difficulties or the other caller isn't answering. Select the Close Conversation button (at the top of the Chat window) to close the message panel.

5. Select the red End Call button to complete your call.

6. When someone calls you, the Incoming Call panel appears, as shown in **Figure 8-16**. Select Turn Video On (at the bottom of the panel) to initiate the call.

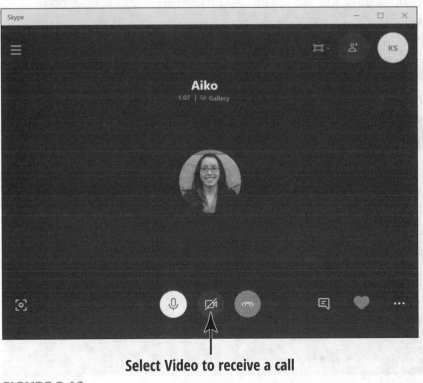

Select Video to receive a call

FIGURE 8-16

Ask Questions of Cortana

1. Click or tap the Talk to Cortana button (it looks like a circle) on the left side of the taskbar. As soon as you click or tap, a "digital assistant" called Cortana springs to life, as shown in **Figure 8-17, left.** Cortana can respond to questions you ask with your voice.

TIP

To use Cortana, your computer's microphone must be up and running. Turn to Chapter 13 if the microphone on your computer isn't connected or working properly.

2. Say aloud, "Tell me a joke." As you say these words, they appear in the text box, and if all goes right, Cortana recites a joke. As well, the words of the joke appear on the screen, as shown in **Figure 8-17, right.**

3. Say the words "Hey, Cortana," and ask, "What is the weather in Chicago, Illinois?" Cortana gives you the weather in Chicago.

TIP

Ask questions of Cortana while the word *Listening* appears in the box. Seeing this word tells you that Cortana is prepared to field a question.

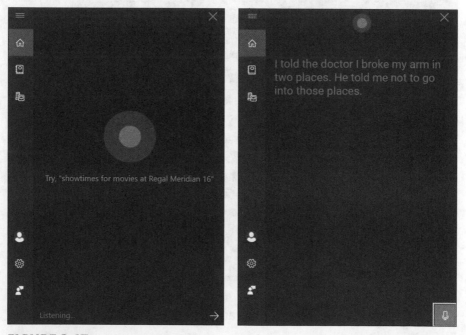

FIGURE 8-17

4. Ask aloud, "What is the safest car?" As shown in **Figure 8-18,** Cortana quickly searches the Internet and provides an answer. Regardless of whether Cortana can answer a question well, you can always select the See More Results on Bing.com link in Cortana to open your browser to the Bing website and conduct a search there.

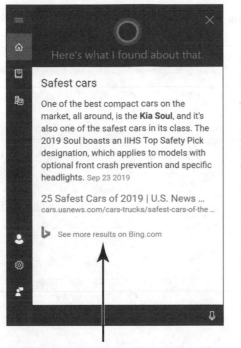

Click to search the Internet

FIGURE 8-18

5. Cortana can remind you to attend events and appointments. Say, "Remind me." Cortana replies, "Sure thing, what should I remind you about?" or "What do you want to remember?" Meantime, you see a Cortana panel like the one in **Figure 8-19.** Next, say "Walk the dog." Cortana asks when you want to be reminded. Reply, "In five minutes," and answer "yes" when Cortana asks you to confirm that you want to be reminded. As long as you begin by saying "Remind me," Cortana can record reminders like this.

6. On the Cortana App bar, select the Notebook button and then select the Reminders button (the light bulb). You go to the Reminders screen. You see the reminder to walk the dog.

Say "remind me" to record a reminder

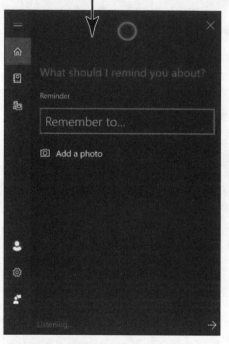

FIGURE 8-19

3
Having Fun with Windows 10

IN THIS PART . . .

Find and purchase apps at the Microsoft Store.

Take and edit photos and videos.

Play music and watch videos.

Chapter 9

Exploring the Microsoft Store

You can do many things with Windows 10, such as send email, browse the web, play games, and look at photos and videos. You can read the news and chat with family and friends. All these functions and more involve computer programs. Back in the day, such programs were called *applications.* Now, we call them *apps.*

Windows 10 comes with a few apps installed, such as the Weather and Maps apps. (See Chapter 2 for information on using these two apps and apps in general.) To obtain other apps — free or otherwise — you use the Microsoft Store.

To install an app from the Microsoft Store, you need a Microsoft Account. See Chapter 4 for information on setting up a Microsoft Account.

Microsoft tests and approves all apps in the Microsoft Store. For quality and security purposes, you can install Windows 10 apps only from the Microsoft Store.

In this chapter, you peruse the apps and games in the Microsoft Store, including those already installed on a new machine. You install a new game, discover how to manage the apps and games you own, and see how to rate and review an app or game. Finally, you find out how to make sure that the Microsoft Store can receive payments in case you want to buy an app or game.

Explore Apps and Games by Category

1. On the Start screen, select the Store tile.

2. Look over the Store home screen, shown in **Figure 9-1.** The home screen shows top-rated apps and games, as well as apps and games that Microsoft thinks you will be interested in based on your previous purchases, if you made any. Notice the navigation bar along the top of the screen (see **Figure 9-1**). It offers five choices: Home, Gaming, Entertainment, Productivity, and Deals. Wherever your travels take you in the Store, the navigation bar appears along the top of the screen so that you can return to the home screen or redirect your search for apps, games, entertainment, and whatnot.

TIP

You can also navigate in the Store by selecting the Back button in the upper-left corner of the screen. Selecting this button returns you to the previous screen you were looking at.

3. Select Productivity on the navigation bar to go to the Productivity screen, and then scroll toward the bottom of the screen. As you scroll downward, you see apps, games, and other items that Microsoft recommends for you.

4. Items on the Productivity screen (as well as the other screens) are presented under different headings, including Best Selling Apps and Favorite Apps. Select the Show All button next to the Best Selling

Apps heading, as shown in **Figure 9-2.** Select the Show All button when you want to investigate all the items listed under a particular heading, After you select this button, you see a screen for refining your search, as shown in **Figure 9-3**.

Navigation bar

FIGURE 9-1

5. In the Charts drop-down menu on the left side of the screen, select Top Free to see apps that you can install for free (see **Figure 9-3**). On the Category drop-down menu, select Education to see educational games. Use the Charts and Category menus to refine your searches. They are available wherever you travel in the Store app.

6. Select Gaming on the navigation bar and scroll to the bottom of the Games screen. You pass the familiar Best Selling and Favorite headings. You can select the Show All button next to a heading to investigate all games in a heading. The Gaming screen works just like the Productivity screen.

Show All button

FIGURE 9-2

7. Return to the Store home screen using one of these methods:

- **Back button:** Click or tap the Back button (or press the Backspace key) as many times as necessary to return to the home screen. This button is located in the upper-left corner of the screen.

- **Navigation bar:** Select Home on the navigation bar (refer to **Figure 9-1**).

TIP

Did you see an app or game you want to acquire as you completed these steps? If so, skip to "Install a New App or Game," later in this chapter.

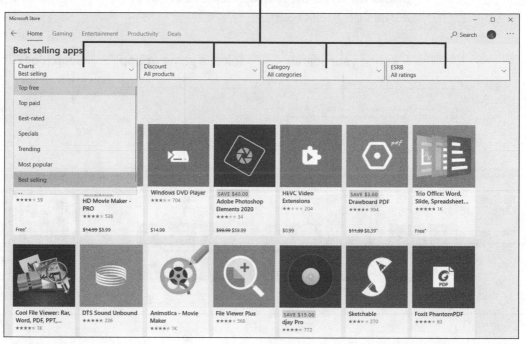

Refine your search

FIGURE 9-3

Search for an App or Game by Name

1. On any Store screen, click in the Search box. This box is in the upper-right corner of the screen, as shown in **Figure 9-4.**

2. Type **chess** in the Search box and press Enter. As shown in **Figure 9-4,** games and apps with the word *chess* in their names appear in the Results screen. The Results screen tells you how many games and apps match your search. After this initial search, you can turn the search in different directions:

   • **Refine the search:** Select Games in the Departments drop-down menu to narrow the search results to games. As well, you can open the Available On drop-down menu and choose PC, Xbox, or another option that describes the platform where you prefer to play games.

- **Show all apps or games:** Select a Show All link to see only apps or games on the screen.

Refine your search   Select a game or app   Search box

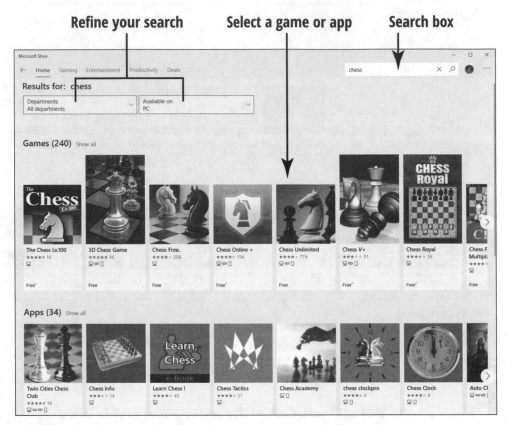

FIGURE 9-4

3. Select Games in the Departments drop-down menu to see games with *chess* in their titles, as shown in **Figure 9-5.** Notice that the refine options have changed. For example, now you can select a category in the Category drop-down menu to narrow the search results to games in a particular category.

4. Proceed to the next section, "Install a New App or Game," or return to the home screen.

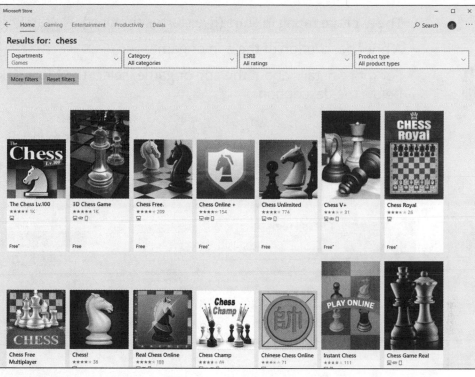

Microsoft Store

Home   Gaming   Entertainment   Productivity   Deals

Search   ⋯

Results for: chess

Departments	Category	ESRB	Product type
Games	All categories	All ratings	All product types

More filters   Reset filters

The Chess Lv.100
★★★★★ 1K
Free*

3D Chess Game
★★★★★ 1K
Free

Chess Free.
★★★★☆ 209
Free

Chess Online +
★★★★★ 154
Free*

Chess Unlimited
★★★★★ 774
Free

Chess V+
★★★★☆ 31
Free*

Chess Royal
★★★★☆ 26
Free*

Chess Free Multiplayer

Chess!
★★★★★ 36

Real Chess Online
★★★★★ 188

Chess Champ
★★★★★ 69

Chinese Chess Online
★★★★☆ 71

Instant Chess
★★★★☆ 111

Chess Game Real

FIGURE 9-5

Install a New App or Game

1. In the Store, search for the Chess Free game. (See the section "Search for an App or Game by Name" for details.) Then select this game on the Results screen.

2. The screen shown in **Figure 9-6** appears. This (and any) game or app screen offers lots of information.

   TIP

   The Back button (left-pointing arrow) on the left side of the navigation bar takes you back to the previously viewed screen.

3. On the top half of the screen, note the following:

   • The Get/Price button (don't click it just yet). This button is called Get if the game is free; otherwise, the button lists the cost of the app or game.

- The average rating in stars (five stars is the best).

- A brief description of the app or game.

TIP

For more details about the app or game, select the More link below the description.

Rating   Select to install

FIGURE 9-6

4. On the bottom half of the screen, note the following:

- A thorough description of the app or game.

- Screenshots that show what the app or game looks like onscreen.

- Additional information, including the age rating and release date.

5. To read reviews by users, select the Reviews link. You see the reviews that Microsoft deems most useful.

6. Select the Get button to download and install Chess Free. Because the game costs nothing, the button reads "Get."

7. If you're not already signed in, enter your Microsoft Account email address and password on the screen that pops up. Then select Sign In.

TIP

Many apps are free. Before you buy an app, see the section "Add Billing Information to the Microsoft Store."

TIP

If you purchase an app, you are buying a license to install that app on up to five machines using the same Microsoft Account. The Microsoft Store will track how many times and on which machine the app is installed.

8. The download indicator appears and a progress bar shows the game being downloaded and installed. When the installation is complete, the words *This product is installed* appear below the game's name. What's more, the message *Chess Free just got installed, check it out* appears in a pop-up message in the lower-right corner of the computer screen. (Select the Notifications button in the lower-right corner of the Windows screen to see this message if you missed it.)

TIP

Installing an app may take a few seconds or a few minutes. You can do anything while an app installs — except use the app.

TIP

If you don't see *This product is installed,* the app may still be installing. If after a few minutes you still don't see this message, select the Get button again.

9. To play Chess Free or to use any game or app after you install it, select the Start button. You may see the recently installed app on the Start menu under Recently Added, as shown in **Figure 9-7, left.** If you don't see it there, start your game or app the conventional way — by looking for the game or app in the alphabetical list (refer to **Figure 9-7, right**). If you haven't used an app yet, the word New appears below its name, as shown in the figure. Select the game or app's tile on the Start menu to open the game or app.

TIP

You can move the Chess Free tile to the Start screen. See Chapter 3 for information on rearranging tiles on the Start screen.

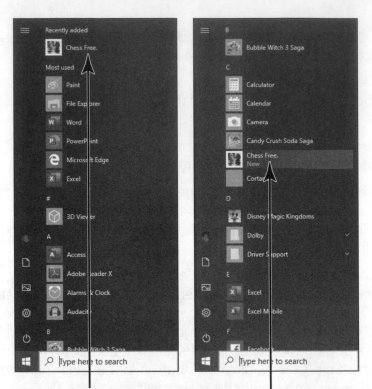

Look for recently installed apps here

The word New appears under recently installed apps

FIGURE 9-7

Examine Your Apps and Games

1. To see which apps and games you have, select the See More button. This button (look for the three dots) is located to the right of the Search box, as shown in **Figure 9-8.** A drop-down menu appears after you select the See More button. This drop-down menu is the place to start when examining, updating, rating, and uninstalling apps and games.

2. Choose My Library on the See More drop-down menu (refer to **Figure 9-8**). The My Library screen appears, as shown in **Figure 9-9.**

3. Scroll to see which apps you have or open the All Types drop-down menu and select an option to see apps or games only. For each game or app, you see an icon and the name of the game or app.

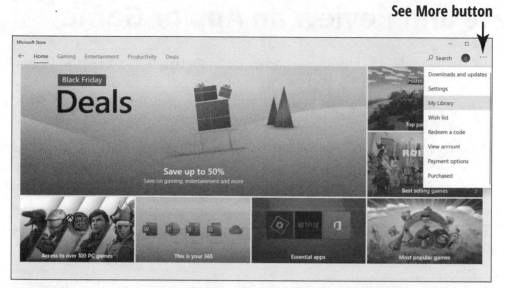

FIGURE 9-8

FIGURE 9-9

Rate and Review an App or Game

1. On the My Library screen (refer to **Figure 9-9**), select the Chess Free game. If you don't have this game, see the section "Install a New App or Game," earlier in this chapter, or substitute any app or game you have installed.

2. In the Chess Free window, select the Reviews link. You see reviews, as shown in **Figure 9-10.** Select the Rate and Review button. The review screen appears (refer to **Figure 9-10**). Every app and game has a Rate and Review button.

> You can rate or review only apps and games that you've installed, and you must be signed in with your Microsoft Account.

TIP

FIGURE 9-10

3. In the review screen, choose the number of stars you want to give this game. (Select one star for the lowest rating; select five for the highest rating.) Select the Add a Review button.

4. In the Write Your Review screen, say what you will, up to 500 characters, including spaces and punctuation.

5. In the Headline box, type a summary or overview of your comments, such as *Great app* or *Needs work*.

TIP

Your comments may help another person decide whether to install an app. In addition, the app's developer may use customer feedback to fix problems or add features.

Your Microsoft Account name and picture, if you have one — but not your email address — appear with your review.

TIP

6. Select the Submit Now button when you're done with your review.

Add Billing Information to the Microsoft Store

1. To add the billing information necessary to buy apps and games, select the See More button (refer to **Figure 9-8**) and select Purchased on the drop-down menu. Your browser opens to the Order History page of your Microsoft Account records.

TIP

See Chapter 4 for information on creating a Microsoft Account.

2. For security purposes, Microsoft asks you to enter your email address and password on the next screen. Enter your password and select the Sign In button.

3. Scroll through the screen to make sure that the information here is accurate. If you are not being billed to the correct credit card or you want to change the credit card to which you are billed, select Payment & Billing on the toolbar and choose Payment Options on the drop-down menu that appears.

4. Select a payment method (or select Edit Info if Microsoft already has credit card information on you) and do the following:

   • Select your credit card type.

   You must fill out all parts of this form except for Address Line 2.

- Enter your credit card number in the box provided. Don't enter dashes or spaces.

- Under Expiration Date, select the month (MM) and year (YYYY) your card expires.

- Enter your name as it appears on your credit card.

- Under CVV, enter the three- or four-digit verification code from your credit card. (Select What's This? for an illustration of the location of this code on your card.)

5. In the Billing Address section, do the following:

- Enter your street address, city, state, and ZIP Code.

- Select your Country/region.

- Under Phone Number, enter your area code in the first box and the remainder of your number in the second box.

6. When you're ready to continue, select Save.

7. If any of your data is incomplete or invalid, the form remains onscreen. Look for indications of a problem. Review each entry before selecting Submit.

8. If your information was accepted, you return to the Your Account screen. Under Payment and billing info, note your credit card type, the last four digits of your number, and the expiration date.

Chapter **10**

Taking Photos and More

Windows 10 makes enjoying digital photos easy. You can pick and choose photos to look at or display a group of photos in a slide show. You set a favorite photo to be your Lock screen background so that you see it every time you start Windows 10.

If you have a printer, you can print photos for yourself or to send to someone. Even black-and-white prints of color photos may be nice. If you have a scanner, you can even scan photos to make digital copies of photographs that as yet exist only in paper form.

Of course, if you want to take your own photos, nothing beats having a digital camera. Copy photos from your camera to your Pictures folder for viewing and sharing. Or use the Camera app with the built-in camera found in many laptops and tablets.

In this chapter, you use the tools that come with Windows 10 for working with, printing, scanning, and editing photos.

Take Photos (and Videos) with Your Computer

1. Select the Camera app on the Start screen. If you don't have a web-cam, the app screen displays *We can't find your camera.* If you don't have a built-in webcam, or the resolution of the one you have is too low, you can easily add a webcam. Simply plug the camera into your computer — it's that easy.

You can choose from many good webcam models. Generally, get the highest video resolution you can afford, because you'll probably use the camera for video chats. Consider the size of the camera, its attachment to your computer, and whether it has a microphone (you definitely need a microphone).

For instructions about opening apps such as the Camera app, visit Chapter 2.

2. The first time you use the Camera app, the screen displays *Let Windows camera access your location?* Select Yes to continue. (If you don't want to continue, don't choose No unless you never expect to use this app. Instead, simply switch back to the Windows desktop.)

3. The Camera app opens, and there's a good chance you recognize the face staring back at you. Very likely the face isn't wearing a hat and dark glasses like the debonair guy in **Figure 10-1.** To take a photo, smile and then click or tap the Take Photo button (it's on the right side of the screen). You may hear a shutter click. Your photo is placed automatically in a folder called Camera Roll in the Pictures folder.

Select the Camera Roll icon in the lower-right corner of the Camera app to view the photo you most recently took. After that, you can select See All Photos to open the Photos App and view photos there. (Select the Back button in the upper-left corner of the screen to resume taking photos.)

4. To take a time-lapse photo, use the Photo Timer button on the left side of the screen. Select this button one, two, or three times to tell the Camera app to wait 2, 5, or 10 seconds before taking the photo. Then click or tap the Camera button and wait 2, 5, or 10 seconds for the photo to be taken.

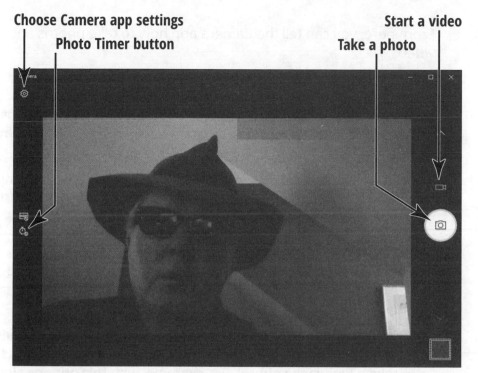

Choose Camera app settings

Photo Timer button

Start a video

Take a photo

FIGURE 10-1

5. Select the Video button (shown in **Figure 10-1**). Nothing happens until you click or tap the Video button a second time, at which point you're in moving pictures. A counter indicates the length of the video. Short is sweet in video. You can speak, too. Click or tap the Video button to stop the video. As with photos you take with the Camera app, videos are saved initially in the Camera Roll subfolder of the Pictures folder. Select the Camera button to turn off the video function and return to taking still photos (with the next click or tap).

Leave the Camera app open to explore the Camera settings, which I explain next.

Choose Camera Settings

1. If the Camera app isn't open, open it now. Then select the Settings button located in the upper-left corner of the Camera window (refer to **Figure 10-1**). The Settings panel opens, as shown in **Figure 10-2**.

From here, you can tell the Camera app how to take photos and videos.

2. Turn Pro Mode on if you want to choose a brightness setting for your photos. After you turn on Pro Mode, a Brightness icon appears on the left side of the Camera app screen. Selecting this icon makes a slider appear so that you can adjust the brightness of photos from 100 percent (very bright) to 0 percent (very dark).

3. Choose a Framing Grid option to help aim the camera. For example, the Crosshairs option places crossing lines in the center of the screen so that you know where the center of your photos will be.

4. Under Photos, decide how you want to take photos:

- **Photo quality:** These options determine the aspect ratio and size of photos in pixels. For example, you can shoot narrow (the 4:3 options) or widescreen (the 16:9 options) photos.

- **Time lapse:** Choose this option when you want to take a series of time-lapse photos (the previous topic in this chapter explains how to take a time-lapse photo). For example, with this option selected and the Photo Timer set to 2 seconds, the Camera app takes a time-lapse photo every 2 seconds until you click or tap the Camera button a second time, which tells the app to stop taking photos.

5. Under Videos, decide how you want to take videos:

- **Video recording:** These options determine the aspect ratio and the number of pixels that appear in video frames. Notice that the fps (frames per second) setting in each option is the same, 30. *Aspect ratio* refers to the proportional relationship between a video's width and height. The most common aspect ratios are 16:9 (widescreen) and 4:3 (old-fashioned TV). A *pixel* is one point of color. Suffice it to say, the more pixels in the setting, the clearer the video is.

- **Flicker reduction:** These options reduce the flickering that can occur when video is taken under fluorescent light. The 50 Hz (hertz) setting applies to the U.S. and Canada, where the AC (alternating electrical current) runs at 50 Hz; the 60 Hz setting applies to rest of the world.

FIGURE 10-2

6. Return to the Camera app by clicking or tapping the Camera app screen.

7. Return to the Start screen. See the section "View Photos with the Photos App" to see and maybe edit the photos you just took.

Copy Photos from Your Camera

1. If your digital camera came with a cable, connect that cable to the camera, connect the other end of the cable to a USB port on your computer, and turn your camera on. If your laptop or tablet has a built-in card slot, you can take the memory card out of the camera and insert it in that slot.

TIP

2. If your computer doesn't have a built-in card slot, consider buying a small memory card reader that plugs into your computer and works with your camera's memory card. You don't need a multicard reader, just a reader with a single slot the size of your camera card. I consider a card reader to be more convenient than using a cable.

TIP

The techniques described here for importing photos from a camera also apply to videos. Follow these steps as well to copy videos from your digital camera to your computer.

3. Windows 10 detects your camera and may briefly display a notification indicating *Select to choose what happens with this device.* If you're quick enough to tap or click this notification, Windows 10 displays your choices, as shown in **Figure 10-3.** Select Open Device to View Files, if that option is available, to open File Explorer to the photos on your camera, as shown in **Figure 10-4 (top).** Then skip to Step 4. If you didn't catch the notification in time or you didn't see the notification, continue to Step 4 to import photos another way.

TIP

See Chapter 3 for information on increasing the time a notification remains onscreen.

Canon PowerShot ELPH 100...

Choose what to do with this device.

Import photos and videos
Photos

Import photos and videos
OneDrive

Open device to view files
File Explorer

Take no action

FIGURE 10-3

4. Select the File Explorer icon on the taskbar to start File Explorer. Then look for and select your camera in the Folders panel on the left side of the screen (refer to **Figure 10-4, top**). Your camera is located under *This PC* in the Folder pane.

TIP

See Chapter 14 for detailed information about using File Explorer.

5. In File Explorer, select the photos you want to copy from your camera to your computer. Depending on your camera setup, the photos may be in a subfolder (refer to **Figure 10-4, top**). Use these techniques to select the photos:

   - Hold down the Ctrl button and click or tap photos to select them individually.

   - Press Ctrl+A to select all the photos in a folder.

6. Copy the photos you selected so that you can paste them into a folder on your computer. Use one of these techniques to copy the photos:

   - Press Ctrl+C.

   - On the Home tab in File Explorer, select the Copy button.

7. In File Explorer, select the folder where you want to copy your photos.

TIP

If you want to be able to view and edit your photos with the Photos app, select the Pictures folder or one of its subfolders, as shown in **Figure 10-4 (bottom)**, and copy the photos there.

TIP

Organizing photos can be a challenge. If you dump more than a few dozen photos into the Pictures folder without using folders, finding a specific photo later will be difficult. Using folders with unintelligible names doesn't help, either. Most of my folder names are based on the year and month (such as 2020–06) or the subject, such as Luke the Lovehound.

8. Paste the photos into the folder you selected in Step 7. Use one of these techniques:

   - Press Ctrl+V.

   - On the Home tab in File Explorer, select the Paste button.

Select your camera (or one of its subfolders)

Copy to the Pictures folder (or one of its subfolders)

FIGURE 10-4

TIP

If you often import photos from a digital camera or memory card, you can speed the process by telling Windows to open File Explorer immediately when you attach your camera or memory card to your computer. On the Start menu, choose Settings and type **autoplay** in the Find a Setting box. In the Search Results panel, select AutoPlay Settings. The AutoPlay window opens, as shown in **Figure 10-5.** In the Memory Card and Camera sections, choose Open Folder (or Open Device) to View Files (File Explorer).

The following is a screenshot of the AutoPlay Settings window:

Settings

□ Home

Find a setting

Devices

▣ Bluetooth & other devices

🖶 Printers & scanners

◯ Mouse

⌨ Typing

✎ Pen & Windows Ink

◉ AutoPlay

▯ USB

AutoPlay

Use AutoPlay for all media and devices

On

Choose AutoPlay defaults

Removable drive

Take no action

Memory card

Choose a default

Canon PowerShot ELPH 100 HS

Open device to view files (File Explorer)

Related settings

Default app settings

🔍 Get help

✐ Give feedback

FIGURE 10-5

View Photos with the Photos App

1. To see photos on your computer, select the Photos app on the Start screen. The Photos screen opens to the Collection window, as shown in **Figure 10-6.** It shows the contents of the Pictures folder (and its subfolders) on your computer. Your screen will look different.

2. If you don't see any pictures, skip to one of the following sections:

- If you have a digital camera, see "Copy Photos from Your Camera."

- If your computer has a built-in camera or a webcam, see "Take Photos (and Videos) with Your Computer."

3. If you see pictures, either scroll down or drag the timeline on the right side of the screen to see more photos. Photos are presented by the dates on which they were taken.

You can take a screenshot — a picture of the current screen — by pressing ▉+Print Screen. (A touchscreen or mouse equivalent is not available.) The screen dims slightly to indicate the capture, which is stored automatically in the Screenshots folder in your Pictures folder. Use this technique to create your own documentation of problems or something you want to see again later.

TIP

4. Select the View Large, View Medium, and View Small button. These buttons are located in the upper-right corner of the screen (refer to **Figure 10-6**). Use them to examine and locate photos.

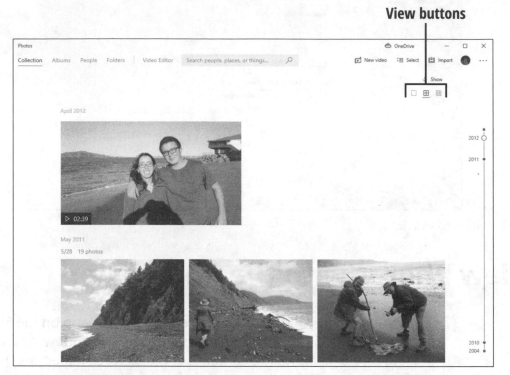

FIGURE 10-6

5. Select any photo to display it full size in the Photos app window, as shown in **Figure 10-7.** When looking at a single photo, you can scroll from photo to photo by selecting the Previous or Next button or by clicking or tapping the right edge or left edge of the screen. You can also press the PageDown key (forward) or PageUp key (back).

6. Select the See More button (the three dots on the right side of the App bar; refer to **Figure 10-7**) and select Slide Show on the menu that appears. The photos appear in succession. Stop the slide show by clicking or tapping a photo.

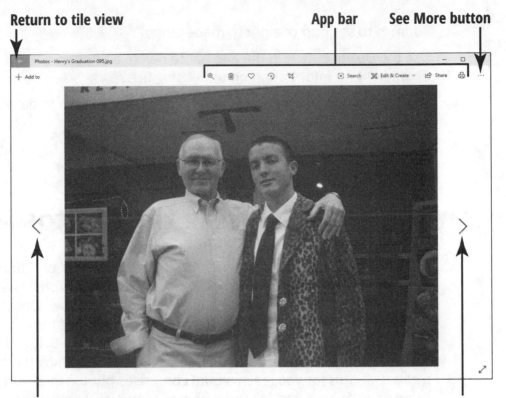

Return to tile view   **App bar**   **See More button**

Previous button
FIGURE 10-7

Next button

TIP

Select the See More button on the right side of the app bar to display some new commands — Open With, Copy, Set As, and File Info, to name a few. By selecting File Info, you can see each photo's name, when it was taken, and its file size.

7. Zoom in and out on a photo using one of these methods (repeat to zoom in or out more):

- **Mouse:** Click the Zoom button at the top of the screen. A slider appears. Drag the slider to the left to shrink the photo; drag the slider to the right to enlarge the photo.

- **Touchscreen:** Touch two fingers on the screen. Move your fingers apart to zoom in. Pinch your fingers closer together to zoom out.

- **Keyboard:** Press Ctrl+plus sign (actually, press the equals sign — no need to press the Shift key) to zoom in. Press Ctrl+minus sign to zoom out.

TIP

Zoom in to see part of a photo made larger.

Use the Delete button in the app bar to delete a photo. See Chapter 14 for information on undeleting files.

8. Select the arrow on the left side of the app bar to return to tile view. In this view, you can see more than one photo.

TIP

The Photos app offers many options for editing photos. See "Edit Photos Using the Photos App," later in this chapter.

Organizing Photos Using the Photos App

1. In the Photos app, photos are organized by date in the Collection window (refer to **Figure 10-7**), but you can organize photos other ways as well, starting in the Albums, People, or Folders window. Organize photos so that you can find and view them easily. Select the Albums tab to open the Albums window, as shown in **Figure 10-8.** If you've already spent some time with the Photos app, the app may have created albums for you (each album comprises photos taken on the same day). If you asked for some photos to be "favorites" (I show you how shortly), the Photos app creates a Favorites album so that you can view these photos.

2. Select New Album to create a new album for storing photos. The Create New Album window opens (see **Figure 10-8**). Scroll through and select photos you want for your album by selecting the check boxes on photos. Then select the Create button. The Album window opens and you see a slide-show presentation of the photos you selected for the album. Select the Back button to return to the Albums window.

TIP

To remove an album from the Albums window, click or tap to select it. Then select the Remove button. To change an album's cover photo, right-click or tap and hold the album, choose Change Your Photo on the pop-up menu, select a photo in the Choose a Cover Photo window, and select the Done button.

Create a new album   **Select photos**

FIGURE 10-8

3. Select the People tab to open the People window, as shown in **Figure 10-9**. It may interest you to know that Windows 10 facial recognition software is capable of recognizing faces in photos. If you store a number of photos in the Photos app, the People window shows the faces of people that Windows 10 recognizes. By attaching names to the faces that are recognized, you can identify photo subjects by name and in so doing search for photos of people in the Photos app. To attach a name to photos that Windows 10 recognizes, select Add Name below a face (refer to **Figure 10-9**). Then type a name or choose one from the Contacts list that appears, and press Enter.

4. To find photos of someone who is recognized, click or tap in the Search box. A drop-down menu with names appears (refer to **Figure 10-9**). Select a name to see all the person's photos.

Find photos of a named person   **Add a name**

FIGURE 10-9

TIP

If you object to Windows 10 butting into your private life with its facial recognition software, select the See More button in the upper-right corner of the screen and choose Settings on the drop-down menu. Then, in the Settings window, scroll to the People setting and turn the People setting off.

5. Locate and select a photo you particularly like to display it full size. Then select the Add to Favorites button (the heart-shaped button along the top of the screen). Selecting Add to Favorites places a link to the photo in the Favorites album. Select the Back button, visit the Albums tab, and select the Favorites album. You see photos you deemed "favorites." Add a photo to the Favorites folder so that you can find it quickly.

6. Select the Folders tab to open the Folders window. By default, the Photos app keeps track of photos found in the Pictures folder (and its subfolders) on your computer. Suppose you want to manage photos in other folders with the Photos app. Select Add a Folder. The Select Folder dialog box appears. Select a Folder and then select the Add Folder to Pictures button. Photos in the folder you select are now available for viewing in the Photos app.

Edit Photos Using the Photos App

1. You can use the Photos app to change a photo's size or appearance. In the Photos app, click or tap the photo you want to edit so that it fills the screen; then select the Edit & Create button, and choose Edit on the drop-down menu The Editing window opens, as shown in **Figure 10-10.** This window offers many tools for touching up photos. To edit a photo, select a retouching method along the top of the screen (Crop & Rotate, Filters, or Adjustments) and then choose editing options.

2. Using the Filters method, you can take advantage of preset edits to photographs. After you select Filters, filter presets appear on the right side of the screen (refer to **Figure 10-10, top**). They offer the chance to change the light and color of a photograph in one fell swoop. Drag the Filter Intensity slider at the top of the screen to further change the look of a photograph.

TIP

If you make mincemeat of a photograph and you want the original version back, select the Undo All button. Selecting this button restores a photograph to its original, pristine state.

3. Choose the Adjustments method to alter the brightness and color of your photograph (refer to **Figure 10-10, bottom**). By dragging sliders on the right side of the screen, you can do much to change the appearance of a photo.

4. Many photos can be improved by *cropping,* which involves cutting out distracting elements and keeping just part of the photo. You might crop a photo to concentrate on its most important part. To crop, select the Crop & Rotate method at the top of the screen. Then either select an aspect ratio or choose the Custom aspect ratio and drag the size or corners of the picture box until the photo is to your liking. The box tells you which parts will remain after cropping, as shown in **Figure 10-11.**

TIP

Sometimes when you import photos from a digital camera or scanner, they arrive askew because the photographer turned the camera the wrong way when shooting. You can correct this error by selecting Crop & Rotate and then selecting the Rotate button until the photo turns right-side-up.

Choose an editing method

Save your edits

FIGURE 10-10

5. Select Save a Copy when you finish doctoring your photograph to keep the original photograph as well as the edited version.

FIGURE 10-11

Print Photos Using the Photos App

1. If necessary, connect the cable from your printer to the USB port on your computer and make sure that your printer is turned on.

2. In the Photos app, select the photo you want to print using a click or tap to display the photo at full screen.

3. Select the Print button on the right side of the app bar (it looks like a printer; refer to **Figure 10-7**). The Print window appears, as shown in **Figure 10-12**.

TIP

Here's a handy keyboard shortcut that works in any app: Press Ctrl+P to open the Print window straightaway.

4. Select a printer. Note the preview. Select the Print button.

TIP

Chapter 13 explains printing in detail.

FIGURE 10-12

Scan Photos and Documents

1. Scan photos and documents to preserve them in digital form. Old family photos and heirloom documents such as birth certificates are candidates for scanning. *Scanning* means to render a paper photograph or document as a computer file so that you can post it on the Internet or send it by email. To scan photos and documents, you must have a scanner or a printer that is capable of scanning (most printers have a scanning capability). To start, connect the cable from your scanner or printer to the USB port on your computer. Make sure that your scanner or printer is turned on. If you're using a printer, put it in Scan mode (which probably means pressing the Scan button).

2. Put the item you want to scan in your scanner or printer.

3. Enter the word **scan** in the Search box on the left side of the taskbar. On the pop-up menu that appears, select Windows Fax and Scan. The Windows Fax and Scan application opens.

4. In the navigation window, select Scan and then select the New Scan button. The New Scan dialog box appears (refer to **Figure 10-13**). Starting here, you can tell Windows whether you want a high-quality or low-quality scan. On the Color Format menu, for example, choose Grayscale or Black and White instead of Color if you're scanning a black-and-white document. Choose a Resolution (DPI) higher than 300 to render your photo or document in greater detail.

TIP

Unless you're scanning more than one item, deselect the Preview or Scan Images as Separate Files option. This option creates a separate digital file for each item in your scanner.

5. Select the Preview button. The preview window shows what your photo or document will look like when it is scanned. If you don't like what you see, play with the settings in the New Scan dialog and select the Preview button again.

Select Preview   Select Scan

FIGURE 10-13

6. Select the Scan button when you're ready to scan your document. Your scanned photo or document appears in the Windows Fax and Scan window with the generic filename "Image."

7. Select your newly scanned image and then select the Save As button. The Save As dialog box appears. Enter a descriptive name for the item, choose a folder to store it in, and select the Save button.

Chapter 14 explains how to save files.

Chapter **11**

Enjoying Music and Videos

The term *media* on computers refers to something other than text. Audio and video are examples of media. *Audio* is a catchall term for music and other sound files, such as books on CD. *Video* includes files that you can shoot with your digital camera as well as Hollywood blockbusters.

The delivery of music has come a long way from Edison's wax cylinder or even vinyl LPs. Nowadays, music is entirely digital. The Groove Music app lets you play your music collection and makes it easy to explore new music. Use Windows Media Player to play audio CDs, to copy audio files to your computer, and to burn songs onto a CD.

The Movies & TV app is similar to the Groove Music app, but it's for video instead of music. You can use it to play your homemade videos.

In this chapter, you play a music CD, copy CDs to your computer for easier access, and burn a CD. You also explore the Groove Music and Movies & TV apps. Finally, you discover how to make a voice recording.

You'll need a different app to play DVDs. Search Microsoft Store for Media Center or for a DVD player app. See Chapter 9 for more information on Microsoft Store.

Popular alternatives for music or videos include Hulu, iTunes, Netflix, and YouTube. All of these are accessible through the web browser. Search Microsoft Store for related apps.

Play and Copy Music from a CD

1. If you have a CD or DVD disc drive or slot on your computer, insert a music CD, label side up for horizontal drives. (Vertical drives are less predictable.)

2. Windows 10 detects your CD and may briefly display this notification: *Choose what to do with audio CDs*. If you're quick enough to tap or click the first notification, Windows 10 displays your choices, as shown in **Figure 11-1.** Select Windows Media Player and then skip to Step 5.

See Chapter 3 for information on increasing the time a notification remains onscreen.

3. If you missed the notification, go to the desktop and select the File Explorer icon (which looks like a folder) in the taskbar.

DVD RW Drive (D:) Audio CD

Choose what to do with audio CDs.

Rip Audio CD
Power2Go

Play Audio CD
PowerDVD 14

Play audio CD
Windows Media Player

Take no action

FIGURE 11-1

4. In the panel on the left side of File Explorer, select your CD drive or DVD drive. You may see the words *Audio CD* or *DVD Drive* in the panel.

5. On the Ribbon, select the Manage tab under Drive Tools. Then select AutoPlay. As shown in **Figure 11-1,** the notification from Step 1 reappears (and stays onscreen until you select something). Select Windows Media Player.

6. If you see the Welcome to Windows Media Player screen, select Recommended Settings and then select Finish. The Windows Media Player plays your music.

7. For access to more options, select Switch to Library, the small button under the X in Windows Media Player, as shown in **Figure 11-2.**

FIGURE 11-2

8. Note the following controls at the bottom of the Windows Media Player, as shown in **Figure 11-3:**

   • **Shuffle:** Select this button to turn on *shuffle,* which randomly mixes the tracks you play. Select again to turn off shuffle, and the tracks play in the order in which they appear onscreen.

   • **Repeat:** Select this button to play all the tracks again after all have played. Select again to turn off the repeat function.

- **Stop:** Select to stop playing.

- **Previous:** Select this button to skip to the previous track. Select and hold to rewind to an earlier point in the track.

- **Play/Pause:** Select the button with two vertical lines to pause play mid-track. Select the same button (now with a triangle pointing to the right) to resume playing from the point you paused.

- **Next:** Select this button to skip to the next track. Select and hold to fast-forward through the track.

- **Mute/Unmute:** Select this button to silence the player. Although the track continues to play, you won't hear it. When Mute is on, a red circle with a slash appears next to the speaker icon. Select the button again to hear the track.

- **Volume:** Drag the slider to the left to decrease or to the right to increase the volume of the track. Your speakers may also have a manual volume control. Windows 10 has a separate volume control in the taskbar, as well.

- **Switch to Now Playing:** You select this button, which is located in the lower-right corner of the window, to reduce the player to a small size (refer to **Figure 11-2**).

9. To copy the CD tracks to your Music library, select Rip CD. This button is located on the toolbar along the top of the screen, as shown in **Figure 11-3**. Ripping a song on a CD takes about a minute. As each song is ripped, the words *Ripped to Library* appear in the Rip Status column of the Windows Media Player.

TIP

If you plan to rip a lot of CDs, select Rip Settings ⇨ Rip CD Automatically and Rip Settings ⇨ Eject CD After Ripping. Just inserting the CD will copy files to your Music library as it plays the CD. Audiophiles should choose Rip Settings ⇨ Audio Quality ⇨ 320 Kbps (Best Quality). As well, audiophiles may consider choosing Format ⇨ WAV, ALAC, or FLAC. These lossless formats are superior to the MP3 format, although fewer devices play files in lossless formats.

10. When the copying process finishes, remove your CD. To play this music in the future, start Windows Media Player, choose Artist, Album, or Genre under Music, select the CD you ripped, select a song title, and select the Play button.

Rip CD button

Windows Media Player

▸ The Essential Bob Wills: 1935-1947 (D:)   Play   Burn   Sync

Organize ▾   Stream ▾   Create playlist ▾   🔘 Rip CD   Rip settings ▾   ▦ ▾ Search   🔍 ▾ ❓

		Album	✓	#	Title	Length	Rip status	Contributing artist	Composer
🖥 Peter Weverka		Audio CD (D:)							
⌄ ▶ Playlists		The Essential Bob ...	✓	1	Osage Stomp	3:04		Bob Wills & His Texas Pl...	B. Wills
▶ Swinging 1960s		Bob Wills & His Tex...	✓	2	Steel Guitar Rag	2:36		Bob Wills & His Texas Pl...	Leon McAuliffe
▶ French		Traditional Country	✓	3	Right Or Wrong	2:56		Bob Wills & His Texas Pl...	Sizemore
▶ My Playlist		1991	✓	4	Time Changes Everything	2:40		Bob Wills & His Texas Pl...	T.A. Duncan
⌄ 🎵 Music		⭐⭐⭐⭐⭐	✓	5	New San Antonio Rose	2:40		Bob Wills & His Texas Pl...	Bob Wills
🎵 Artist			✓	6	Bob Wills Special	2:46		Bob Wills & His Texas Pl...	B. Wills
💿 Album			✓	7	Twin Guitar Boogie	2:44		Bob Wills & His Texas Pl...	A. Shamblin
🎵 Genre			✓	8	Take Me Back To Tulsa	2:42		Bob Wills & His Texas Pl...	Bob Wills
🎞 Videos			✓ ▶	9	A Maiden's Prayer	2:53		Bob Wills & His Texas Pl...	B. Wills
🖼 Pictures			✓	10	Home In San Antone	2:34		Bob Wills & His Texas Pl...	Fred Rose
💿 The Essential Bob Wi			✓	11	Miss Molly	2:36		Bob Wills & His Texas Pl...	C Walker
			✓	12	Texas Playboy Rag	2:39		Bob Wills & His Texas Pl...	B. Wills
🎵 Other Libraries			✓	13	Stay A Little Longer	2:48		Bob Wills & His Texas Pl...	T.A. Duncan
▸ 🎵 10.0.1.3 - Sonos One			✓	14	Roly Poly	2:52		Bob Wills & His Texas Pl...	Fred Rose
🎵 Owner (owner-pc)			✓	15	New Spanish Two Step	2:50		Bob Wills & His Texas Pl...	T.A. Duncan
			✓	16	Sugar Moon	2:17		Bob Wills & His Texas Pl...	C Walker
			✓	17	Brain Cloudy Blues	2:47		Bob Wills & His Texas Pl...	B. Wills
			✓	18	Fat Boy Rag	2:57		Bob Wills & His Texas Pl...	Bob Wills
			✓	19	Deep Water	2:58		Bob Wills & His Texas Pl...	Fred Rose
			✓	20	Bob Will's Boogie	3:05		Bob Wills & His Texas Pl...	Kelso

Media changing...   🔀 🔁 | ⏹ | ⏮ ⏮ (▶) ▶▶| ◀ ━━━●━━━   ⇶

Control music playback   **Switch to Now Playing**

FIGURE 11-3

💡
TIP

Songs you rip from a CD are kept on your computer in a subfolder of the Music folder. To copy or move music that you ripped from a CD, open the Music folder, open the subfolder named after the CD you ripped, and copy or move the files.

💡
TIP

You can play anything in the Music library by using the Groove Music app. See the next section, "Listen to the Groove Music App."

💡
TIP

Pin the Windows Media Player to the taskbar for easy access: Click the right mouse button over the icon in the taskbar, or tap and hold until a box appears and then release. On the menu that pops up, select Pin to Taskbar. You can also search for Windows Media Player on the Start screen. See Chapter 2 for information on pinning apps to the Start screen.

TIP

If your music CD doesn't play automatically the next time you insert one, you can tell Windows 10 how to handle audio CDs. On the Start screen, click or tap Settings and then type **autoplay** on the Settings screen. In the search results, select AutoPlay Settings. The Settings screen opens to the AutoPlay settings. Turn on the Use AutoPlay for All Media and Devices option to make CDs play automatically.

Listen to the Groove Music App

1. Select the Groove Music app on the Start screen. The Groove Music app home screen appears, as shown in **Figure 11-4.** The Groove Music app enables you to play songs that you ripped (copied) from CDs, songs that you purchased from iTunes and other music purveyors, and playlists that you created from songs you own.

TIP

If you see *Can't sign in,* you're not connected through a Microsoft Account. You'll still be able to do the steps in this section, though. You need to sign in only to buy music.

2. Initially, the Groove Music app recognizes music files kept in these folders on your computer: `C:\Users\Your Name\OneDrive\Music` and `C:\Users\Your Name\Music`. Maybe you keep your music files in other folders. To tell the Groove Music app where your music files are, tap or click the Settings button (refer to **Figure 11-4**). In the Settings screen, select the *Choose Where We Look for Music* link. The Build Your Collection dialog box appears, as shown in **Figure 11-5.** Select the Add Folder button, choose a folder in the Select Folder dialog box, and tap or click the Add This Folder to Music button. Then select Done. Repeat these instructions to add all the folders where you store music files.

3. To find the song you want to hear, choose an option in the navigation pane and get to it:

- **Search:** Type the name of an artist, album, or song in the Search box. As you type, suggested matches appear below the Search box. For now, ignore these suggestions (but take advantage of them in the future to save typing). Instead, select the magnifying glass or press Enter. Search results appear.

Locate songs   Settings button

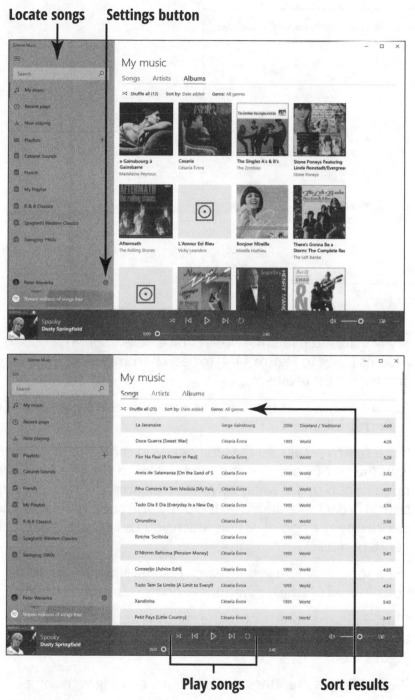

Play songs   Sort results

FIGURE 11-4

Build your collection from your local music files

Right now, we're watching these folders:

+

Music
C:\Users\peter\Music   ✕

French
C:\Music\French   ✕

Swinging 1960s Pop
C:\Music\Swinging 1960s Pop   ✕

Done

FIGURE 11-5

- **My Music:** After you make this choice, select Songs, Artists, or Albums (refer to **Figure 11-4**) to search from a song list, a list of artists, or a list of albums.

- **Recent Plays:** A list of albums you played recently appears. Scroll to find an album.

TIP

If the search results list is a long one, you can narrow your search with the Sort By and Genre options (refer to **Figure 11-4**). Sorting opens a pop-up list whereby you can arrange the results in alphabetical order, date-added order, or by artist or album. Choosing Genre opens a pop-up list on which you can choose a particular genre of music.

4. Select a song or album in the search results. Note the following options (not all of which may appear on the current screen):

- **Play:** Plays the song. Notice the controls at the bottom of the screen for pausing the song and controlling the volume (refer to **Figure 11-4**).

- **Play All:** Plays the songs on the album, starting with song 1.

- **Add To:** Opens a pop-up menu with playlists, and you can add the song to one of those playlists (see "Create and Manage Playlists," the next topic in this chapter).

TIP

You can listen to music as you conduct a search. To return to the song or album that is currently playing, select the Now Playing button.

5. To control the volume level on your speakers, use either the volume controls in Groove Music or the Windows 10 volume controls. Select the Speakers icon in the lower-right corner of the Groove Music screen or the Windows 10 screen. A volume slider appears, as shown in **Figure 11-6** (the figure shows the Windows 10 volume controls). Slide the control to adjust the volume. Select the speaker icon on the right side of the slider to mute or unmute all sounds.

Speakers / Headphones (Realtek High Definitio...

10:57 AM
2/17/2020

FIGURE 11-6

6. Switch back to the Start screen. The Groove Music app continues to play. The Groove Music tile on the Start screen displays the album art and title of the current song. Select the Groove Music tile to return to the app.

7. Leave the Groove Music app open if you care to discover how to create a playlist, the next topic in this chapter.

Create and Manage Playlists

1. Create a playlist with the Groove Music app to play your favorite songs — songs from different artists — one after the other. After you create the list, you select it in the Groove Music app to play it. To create a playlist in the Groove Music app, select the Create New Playlist button (a plus sign). You see the Name This Playlist dialog box, shown in **Figure 11-7.** Select the words *Name This Playlist,* enter a descriptive name for your playlist, and select Create Playlist.

FIGURE 11-7

2. The Groove Music App has buttons to add songs to a playlist. Next time you're listening to a song or album and you think, "I like that song; it should be on a playlist," do one of the following to add the song to a playlist, as shown in **Figure 11-8:**

- **Add a song:** Select a song's Add To button and select a playlist on the pop-up menu that appears.

- **Add all the songs on an album:** Select the Add To button on the album name and select a playlist on the pop-up menu.

  See "Listen to the Groove Music App," earlier in this chapter, if you need help finding and listening to music on your computer.

3. To play the songs on a playlist, select the name of the playlist on the left side of the screen. The playlist opens, as shown in **Figure 11-9.** Select the Play All button to play the songs in order from first to last. Of course, you can select any song on the list and select its Play button to play it.

TIP

Add an album

FIGURE 11-8

Add a song

4. To change the order of songs on a playlist or remove a song, follow these instructions:

- **Change the order of songs:** Drag a song higher or lower on the list with your mouse or finger.

- **Remove a song:** Select the Delete from Playlist button.

To delete a playlist, open it. Then select the Delete button.

TIP

FIGURE 11-9

Watch Videos

1. Select the Movies & TV app on the Start screen. Microsoft designed this app for watching movies from the Microsoft Store and for watching homemade videos. To watch homemade videos, select the Personal tab on the menu bar. The Videos screen appears, as shown in **Figure 11-10.** Use the Video screen to watch videos.

2. Unless you store your videos in the `C:\Users\`*Your Name*`\Videos` folder, you don't see any videos. To tell the Video app where you store your videos, select the Add Folders button. You come to the Build Your Collection screen. Select the Add button (the plus sign),

and in the Select Folder dialog box, select the folder where videos are stored and then select the Add This Folder to Video button. Repeat these instructions to add all the folders where you store videos.

Go to the Personal tab

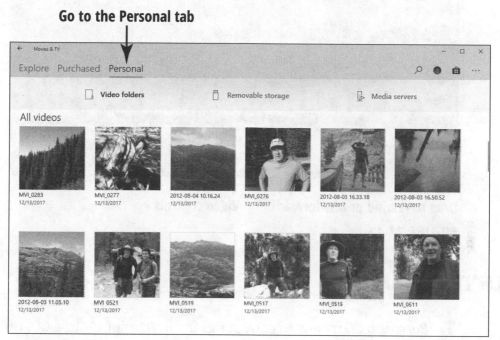

FIGURE 11-10

3. To play a video, select it on the Home screen. It appears in the video player screen, as shown in **Figure 11-11.** Along the bottom of this screen are controls for pausing, playing, and changing the volume level. Drag the slider below the video screen to rewind and fast-forward.

4. Select the Back button (located in the upper-left corner of the screen) to return to the Movies & TV home screen.

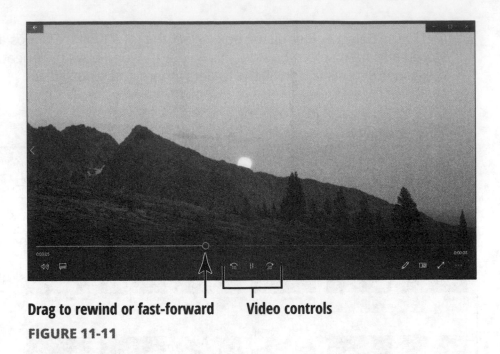

Drag to rewind or fast-forward   **Video controls**

FIGURE 11-11

Burn a CD

1. *Burning a CD* means to copy songs from a computer to a CD. Burn a CD so that you can play the songs on your car's CD player or pass along your favorite songs to a friend. To burn a CD, start by opening Windows Media Player, as shown in **Figure 11-12.**

Earlier in this chapter, "Play and Copy Music from a CD" explains Windows Media Player in detail.

TIP

To burn a CD, your computer needs an *optical disk drive,* a hardware device for playing and recording to CDs and DVDs. If your computer doesn't have one and you want to burn CDs, you can buy optical disk drives that plug into your computer.

TIP

2. Create a playlist so that Windows Media Player knows which songs to burn to the CD. To create a playlist, select the Create Playlist button and enter a name for the playlist where the words *Untitled Playlist* appear. The name you enter then appears under Playlists on the left side of the screen.

3. Locate songs for your playlist and drag and drop their titles one by one onto your playlist name. The words *Add to [Playlist Name]* appear when you drag a song title onto your list. Use these techniques to locate songs so you can drag them in the playlist:

- **Browse for songs:** Under Music, select Artist, Album, or Genre on the left side of the screen (refer to **Figure 11-12**). A list of artists, albums, or genres appears.

- **Change views:** Open the Change Views drop-down menu and choose Icon, Title, or Details to make finding a song title easier.

- **Search for songs:** Enter a search term in the Search box.

Drag titles over the playlist name

Create a playlist   Change views

FIGURE 11-12

4. Select your playlist on the left side of the screen. The songs you selected for the list appear, as shown in **Figure 11-13.** To listen to the songs on a playlist, select its name and click or tap the Play button at the bottom of the screen.

TIP

You can edit a playlist. While the list is playing, place more songs on the list (follow Step 3) or remove songs from the list by right-clicking and choosing Remove from List.

5. After you create a playlist, you can burn it to a CD. With Windows Media Player open, insert a blank CD in your computer's CD or DVD drive. Then select the Burn tab (refer to **Figure 11-13**) and drag a playlist from the left side of the screen to Burn List on the right.

You can change the order of the songs before you burn them onto a CD. Drag song titles up or down the list to change the song order.

TIP

6. Note the Audio CD bar on the right side of the screen. It tells you whether there is enough disc space to burn all the songs on the list. If there is enough space, select the Start Burn button. It can take a few minutes to burn a CD. When the job is complete, your computer ejects the CD. I suggest playing it to see whether the songs copied correctly to the CD. While you're at it, label the CD by writing on it with a felt-tip (not a ballpoint) pen. Label the top of the CD, not the bottom.

Select to burn the songs

FIGURE 11-13

Make a Voice Recording

1. Open the Voice Recorder app to record your voice. As shown in **Figure 11-14,** Voice Recorder lists recordings you already made (if you made any recordings).

TIP

It goes without saying, but your computer needs a built-in microphone or microphone jack for plugging in a microphone if you want to make voice recordings.

TIP

The first time you run Voice Recorder, a dialog box asks, "Let Voice Recorder access your documents library?" Select Yes. To change this later, go to the Settings app.

2. Select the Record button (or press Ctrl+R) to begin a recording. A timer tells you how long your recording is. You can select the Pause/Resume Recording button to temporarily stop a recording. Select the Pause/Resume Recording button again to continue recording.

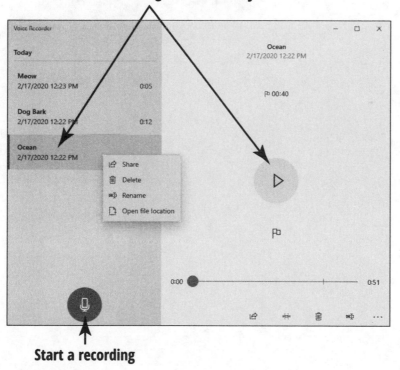

Select a recording and select Play

Start a recording

FIGURE 11-14

3. Select the Stop Recording button (located in the middle of the screen) to end a recording. The name of your recording appears in the list under the generic name *Recording*. To give it a more descriptive name, right-click or tap to display the recording's context menu (refer to **Figure 11-14**), choose Rename, enter a name, and select the Rename button.

TIP To delete a recording, display its context menu and choose Delete.

TIP To access a Sound Recorder file, perhaps to copy or move it, display its context menu (refer to **Figure 11-14**) and choose Open File Location. The Sound Recordings folder opens. From here, you can copy or move the file. See Chapter 14 if you need instructions for handling files.

4

Beyond the Basics

Fine-tune Windows 10.

Manage printers and other peripherals.

Manipulate files and folders.

Keep backup copies of files and folders.

Chapter **12**

Maintaining Windows 10

indows 10 is a bit like a car. To make it run well, you have to maintain it.

Windows 10 uses the Update & Security screen to keep you informed of issues that pertain to your computer's health. The Reliability Monitor can help you pinpoint problems with hardware and software.

Machines such as can openers aren't getting any smarter. Your computer, however, can be programmed to do something it's never done before. To make your computer capable of doing new things, you install new programs. On the other hand, your computer may have some programs that you'll never use and wouldn't miss. You don't have to get rid of them, but doing so is easy enough and can make your computer run better.

In this chapter, you work with the Update & Security screen to check your computer's health status. You also install a program on the desktop and, optionally, uninstall one. This chapter also shows how to make your computer work faster by controlling the startup apps, defragmenting your hard drive, and deleting unnecessary system files. Finally, you discover how to protect your computer against spy-ware, viruses, and other foreign invaders.

Install a New Program on the Desktop

1. You can install software that you download from the web or from a CD or DVD for use on the desktop. (Windows 10 apps must be installed through the Microsoft Store.) In this set of steps, you install Audacity, a free program for editing audio files. To install Audacity, open your browser and enter **audacityteam.org/download** in the address bar. You land on the web page for downloading Audacity. (See Chapter 6 for information on using the Edge browser.)

TIP

If a website offers to install a program automatically, regard that suggestion with suspicion. It may be legitimate or it may be malevolent. Decline downloads from sources that you don't know and trust already.

2. Select the Audacity Installer link to go to the web page for downloading programs.

3. Under Download, select the Audacity Windows Installer link, as shown in **Figure 12-1**.

4. Your browser displays a message at the bottom of the browser window (refer to **Figure 12-1**). Select the Run button. The User Account Control dialog box appears. Select the Yes button to tell Windows you want to download and install the program. In the Select Setup Language dialog box, choose English and select OK.

TIP

Generally, if the installer for a program offers Express or Custom installation options, choose the Express option to let the installer set up the program without further input from you. The Custom or Advanced Settings option allows you to specify where to install the program and, perhaps, which parts of the program to install.

Select Audacity Windows Installer   **Select Run**

FIGURE 12-1

5. In the Setup – Audacity dialog boxes that appear, click Next until you come to the dialog box that asks whether you want to install the program. Select the Install button. In the Information dialog box shown in **Figure 12-2, top,** select the Next button. Last but not least, select the Finish button in the dialog box that tells you that Audacity has finished installing, as shown in **Figure 12-2, bottom.** The Audacity program opens on your screen.

TIP Many programs try to connect to the Internet for updates during installation or when you run the installed program. The first time you run a program, you may be asked whether you want to register the program or configure some aspect of the program. Go with the default (assumed) responses, if you're not sure.

6. Close Audacity. You can do that by selecting the Close button (the X) in the upper-right corner of the screen.

7. Select the Start button to open the Start screen. Audacity appears on the apps list under the letter *A*.

FIGURE 12-2

TIP

To install a program that comes on a CD or DVD, insert the program disc into your computer's disc drive or tray, label side up (or, if your computer has a vertical disc slot, insert the disc with the label side facing left). The AutoPlay dialog box appears. Select the option to run Install or Setup. User Account Control may ask whether you really want to run this program. (Windows 10 tries to keep you from installing software unintentionally by asking for confirmation.)

Remove Desktop Programs

1. Unlike Windows 10 apps from the Microsoft Store, desktop programs are installed and uninstalled directly through the desktop itself. To see which desktop programs are installed, open the Control Panel. Type **control panel** in the Search box (which is located on the left side of the taskbar) and select Control Panel in the Search panel.

TIP

Many of the functions covered in this chapter are part of the Control Panel, which presents many functions for tweaking your computer setup.

2. In the Control Panel window (shown in **Figure 12-3**), under Programs, select Uninstall a Program. (You don't have to uninstall anything; you can simply see what the option offers.) You see the Programs and Features window.

Uninstall a desktop program or just look

FIGURE 12-3

3. The Programs and Features window lists desktop programs, not Windows 10 apps. Initially, these programs are sorted by name. You may want to see the date you last used each program because a program you haven't used in ages may be a candidate for removal. (Otherwise, skip to Step 5.) Use one of the following techniques to display the date last used:

- **Mouse:** Move the mouse pointer over any column heading, such as Name. Click the right mouse button.

- **Touchscreen:** Tap and hold down on any column heading, such as Name. When a box appears around your fingertip, lift your finger.

4. On the context menu that appears, select More. In the Choose Details window (shown in **Figure 12-4**), select Last Used On and then select the OK button. The Last Used On column appears to the right of all the other columns.

Select the Last Used On option

Choose Details   ✕

Select the details you want to display for the items in this folder.

De**t**ails:

☑ Name   Move **U**p
☑ Publisher
☑ Installed On   Move **D**own
☑ Size
☑ Version   **S**how
☑ Last Used On
☐ Comments   **H**ide
☐ Contact
☐ Help Link
☐ Location
☐ Product ID
☐ Readme
☐ Registered Company
☐ Registered Owner
☐ Source

Width of selected column (in pixels):   320

OK   Cancel

FIGURE 12-4

TIP

Before you uninstall a program that you may want to reinstall later, make sure that you have a copy of it on a CD or DVD (or that you know where to download it from the web again). You have no undo option when you uninstall a program.

5. To uninstall a program, select it. For this example, select Audacity, as shown in **Figure 12-5.** You don't have to uninstall Audacity, but if you do, you can follow the steps in the preceding section to reinstall it.

6. Select the Uninstall button (located above the list of program names). Some programs offer the Change and Repair options as well as Uninstall. Repair or Change may be useful for a desktop program that you want to keep but isn't running as expected. When Windows 10 asks whether you really to uninstall, select Yes or No.

Select a program   **Select to uninstall**

![Screenshot of the Programs and Features window in Control Panel showing a list of installed programs with columns for Publisher, Installed On, Size, and Version. Audacity 2.2.1 is highlighted and checked.]

FIGURE 12-5

7. If you uninstalled Audacity or another program, it will no longer appear in the Programs and Features window or on the Start screen.

TIP

Just because you can uninstall a program doesn't mean you should. You can simply ignore programs you don't use. Look at a program's name, publisher, and date installed to determine whether you actually use a program. You may recognize a program you installed recently, as opposed to one installed before you got your computer. If you find that it's more productive to remove large programs than small ones, repeat Steps 3 and 4 to group by size.

TIP

After you install a program, take note of whether your computer runs differently. If your computer slows or behaves sluggishly, the program you recently installed could be the culprit. Uninstall it, if necessary.

Control Startup Apps

1. Startup apps are applications that start running when you turn on your computer. You might be surprised by how many startup apps run in the background without your knowing it. Occasionally you install new software or download a program from the Internet and discover that it runs automatically whether you like it or not. Sometimes the number of startup apps slows the computer down. To see which apps start running automatically when you turn on your computer, start the Task Manager with one of these techniques:

   - **Keyboard:** Press Ctrl+Alt+Del and select Task Manager on the blue screen.

   - **Desktop:** On the Desktop, enter **task** in the Search box and then select the Task Manager tile on the menu that appears.

2. Select More Details (if necessary) in the Task Manager window and then select the Startup tab, as shown in **Figure 12-6.** This is the list of applications that start when your computer starts.

3. Use one of these techniques to open your browser, go on the Internet, and find out what one of these startup applications does:

   - **Mouse:** Right-click an application and choose Search Online.

   - **Touchscreen:** Tap and hold down the name of an application. When a box appears around your fingertip, select Search Online.

4. Notice the Startup Impact column in the Task Manager. Applications with a high impact such as Microsoft OneDrive may be slowing down your computer. If you decide that one of these applications is unwanted or is slowing you down, disable it. (Don't worry, you can enable it later on very easily, as I explain shortly.) To disable an application, select its name in the list and then select the Disable button.

TIP

To enable a startup application in the Task Manager (refer to **Figure 12-6**), select its name and then select the Enable button. The Status column in the Task Manager tells you whether a startup application has been disabled.

Name	Publisher	Status	Startup impact
Adobe Reader and Acrobat ...	Adobe Systems Incorpor...	Disabled	None
CyberLink MediaLibray Servi...	CyberLink	Enabled	Not measured
Lenovo Calliope USB Keybo...	Lenovo	Enabled	Not measured
Lenovo Virtual Camera Servi...	CyberLink Corp.	Enabled	Not measured
Microsoft OneDrive	Microsoft Corporation	Enabled	Not measured
MUI StartMenu Application	CyberLink Corp.	Enabled	Not measured
Send to OneNote Tool	Microsoft Corporation	Enabled	Not measured
Windows Security notificati...	Microsoft Corporation	Enabled	Not measured

FIGURE 12-6

Explore System Information

1. On the desktop, type **control panel** in the Search box. This box is located on the left side of the taskbar. The Search panel appears.

2. Select Control Panel in the Search panel. In the Control Panel, select System and Security.

3. In the System and Security window, select System. The System window shown in **Figure 12-7** appears. This screen is chock-full of information and functions. Note each of the following areas onscreen:

   - **Windows edition:** Of course, you have Windows 10. However, Windows 10 comes in two primary editions: the Home edition, which you are likely to have, and the Pro edition, for computer professionals. You may find information here about so-called Service Packs, which are large collections of updates to Windows 10.

   - **System:** This section displays details about your hardware, including the processor, the amount of installed memory (RAM), and other details.

FIGURE 12-7

- **Computer name, domain, and workgroup settings:** This information pertains to your network, if you have one. If a computer can't connect to a network, the problem is often related to the name of the Workgroup (a network). The Change Settings function lets you change the Workgroup name to match other computers on the same network.

Windows 10 gives your computer a nondescript, generic name to begin with. To give your computer a more descriptive name, select Change Settings in the Computer Name, Domain, and Workgroup Settings section of the System window (refer to **Figure 12-7**). The System Properties dialog box appears. Select the Change button and enter a new name in the Computer Name/Domain Changes dialog box.

- **Windows activation:** In an effort to control software piracy involving bootlegged copies of Windows 10, each copy of Windows 10 must be activated. Odds are that you activated your copy the first time you started your computer. If you don't see *Windows is activated* in this section, select the adjacent link.

TIP

Don't be alarmed by the System information and options. If all goes well, you don't have to use most of what you find here. Some familiarity with this screen will be useful, however, if all doesn't go well later.

Check Your Security and Maintenance Status

1. In the System window (refer to **Figure 12-7**), select Security and Maintenance in the lower-left corner. The Security and Maintenance window appears, as shown in **Figure 12-8**.

TIP

Another way to open the Security and Maintenance window is to type **Security and Maintenance** in the Search box on the Windows taskbar.

FIGURE 12-8

2. Note any message displayed under Review Recent Messages and Resolve Problems. Ideally, you see *No issues have been detected by Security and Maintenance.* If you see a message concerning a specific problem, select that message for more information.

3. Select the Security heading in the Security and Maintenance window. That section expands to detail security functions. Every option should display *On* or *OK.* Here's a brief description of each item under Security:

   - **Network Firewall:** The firewall scans Internet traffic and blocks activity from programs that don't have explicit permission to use Internet access. When you install a program that uses the Internet, you may be asked to approve the connection the first time. The safest practice is to reject online connections that you don't initiate or recognize.

   - **Virus Protection:** Having virus protection for your computer is essential. Windows Defender, an antivirus protection program, comes with Windows 10, although you can install another antivirus program if you want. Later in this chapter, "Protect Your Computer from Viruses and Other Threats" explains how the Windows Defender works.

   - **Internet Security Settings:** These settings pertain to your browser. The default settings may be adequate.

   - **User Account Control:** This function notifies you of programs that try to make changes to your system and requires that you confirm any such changes. In particular, UAC lets you know when a program tries to run or install software that may be malicious. When in doubt, say No or Cancel to UAC messages.

4. Select the Maintenance heading to see what that section includes. Functions under Maintenance consist of the following:

   - **Report problems:** This setting is on, allowing Windows 10 to regularly check for solutions to problems it uncovers. (In Step 5, you run the Reliability History report from this part of the screen.)

   - **Automatic Maintenance:** Your computer automatically performs critical updates, security scans, and diagnostics each day.

TIP

If your computer is in a guest room or bedroom, you may want to change the Automatic Maintenance setting to run maintenance tasks at some time other than the default 3:00 a.m. Your computer may actually wake up at that hour for maintenance (although, if your computer is connected to a power strip, you can turn off the power strip and prevent your computer from turning on automatically in the middle of the night). If the computer can't run maintenance at the appointed hour, it will do so at the next opportunity.

- **File History:** See Chapter 15 for information on using the File History option, which is off by default.

- **Drive status:** *Drives* are hard disks inside or attached to your computer. Your documents, photos, and Windows 10 itself are stored on one or more drives. Ideally, the drive status is *All drives are working properly*. See Chapter 15 for information on backing up and restoring files.

- **Device software:** If a device on your computer needs a driver or other type of software to run properly, you are alerted here (if no drivers are needed, you see the words *No action needed*). Select Install Device Software to install the software.

The Security and Maintenance window is a troubleshooting tool, so you should check it if you have problems running Windows 10.

5. Under Report Problems, select View Reliability History. As shown in **Figure 12-9,** the Reliability Monitor screen graphs your computer's stability and indicates hardware and software problems, including those you may not be aware of. On this screen, red circles indicate critical events such as computer crashes; blue circles are information about software installation and updates; and yellow triangles indicate warnings about noncritical events (something that didn't crash the computer). Select a day in the graph to display details in the lower portion of the screen.

TIP

Reviewing the Reliability Monitor screen helps you distinguish between a one–time glitch and a recurring or worsening problem.

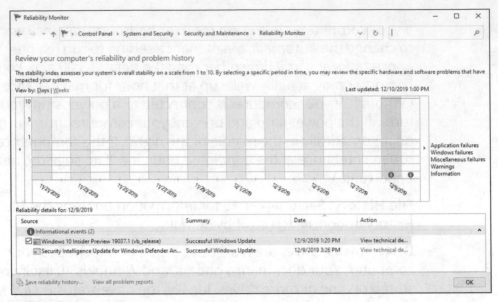

FIGURE 12-9

Speed Up Your Computer

1. Computers are like people — they tend to slow down with age. However, Windows 10 offers a couple of administrative tools that can make your computer work faster. To find out what these tools are, press ⊞+D to go to the desktop and then type **administrative tools** in the Search box. Then select the Windows Administrative Tools tile to open the Administrative Tools area of the Control Panel, as shown in **Figure 12-10.**

2. Select Defragment and Optimize Drives. The Optimize Drives screen opens, as shown in **Figure 12-11.** When you save a file, the new data you recently added gets placed on the hard drive wherever Windows 10 can find room for it. Consequently, a file is stored in many different places. If you've used your computer for a long time, files become fragmented — the bits and pieces are spread all over the drive and your computer has to work hard to assemble all the pieces to open a file.

FIGURE 12-10

FIGURE 12-11

3. Select the C drive and then select the Optimize button. Windows 10 optimizes your hard drive by moving the bits and pieces of files so that they are stored next to each other on the hard drive. It can take a few minutes or a few hours to optimize a hard drive, but no matter, because Windows 10 conducts this activity in the background and you can go on to do other tasks.

4. Return to the Administrative Tools screen (refer to **Figure 12-10**) and select Disk Cleanup. The Disk Cleanup for Windows dialog box appears, as shown in **Figure 12-12.** It tells you how much disk space you can make available on your hard drive by removing unnecessary files.

5. Select the types of files you want deleted, and then select the Clean Up System Files button. A message box appears as the files are deleted from your computer.

FIGURE 12-12

Protect Your Computer from Viruses and Other Threats

1. Windows can identify and remove viruses, spyware, and other male-factors from your computer. To refine how Windows secures your computer against outside threats, press ⊞+D to go to the desktop, type **administrative tools** in the Search box, and then select the Windows Security tile in the Search panel. The Settings app opens to the Windows Security page, as shown in **Figure 12-13.** This page tells you whether the defense mechanisms on your computer are up to date. If they aren't up to date, you can take actions here to update your computer's defenses.

FIGURE 12-13

2. Select Virus & Threat Protection to open the screen shown in **Figure 12-14, top.**

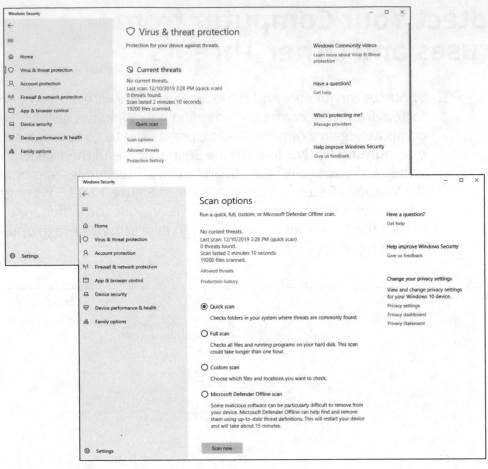

FIGURE 12-14

3. Windows performs "quick scans" in the background each time you run your computer. From time to time, to make sure your computer is thoroughly clean of viruses and spyware, run a full scan. Select the Scan Options link to open the Scan Options window, shown in **Figure 12-14, bottom.** Then make sure that the Full Scan option is selected and select the Scan Now button.

4. A full scan can take a long time as Windows examines all the files on your computer for viruses and spyware. You can do other tasks on your computer while the full scan is running. If Windows finds a bad actor, the file with the virus or spyware is quarantined so that it won't harm your computer.

5. Close the Settings app.

Chapter **13**

Connecting a Printer and Other Devices

E very computer has a screen. Most computers, other than tablets, also have a keyboard and a mouse or other pointing device. You can add a mouse to a laptop that lacks one or replace the keyboard or mouse that came with your computer. Add a printer or a scanner to extend your computer's functionality.

For any hardware add-ons — which tech folk call *peripherals* — Windows 10 has a trick up its sleeve. Thanks to *plug-and-play* technology, which automatically identifies add-on devices, connecting new devices to your computer can be quite easy.

In this chapter, you explore the devices connected to your computer, as well as options available for those devices. You find out how to access devices connected to your computer and also calibrate a touchscreen to make it work better for you.

Trust USB Plug and Play for Hardware

You may find many kinds of add-on devices useful:

» A **printer** lets you, well, print documents and photos. Your choices for printers include black and white versus color, and inkjet versus laser printer. A multifunction printer also works as a copier, scanner, and fax machine.

» A **digital camera** captures photos that you can copy to your computer to enjoy and to share with others. See Chapter 10 for information on working with photos.

» A **scanner** enables you to make digital images of old photos or documents so that you can view them onscreen. Chapter 10 explains how to use a scanner.

» An **external hard drive** stores backup copies of your files. See Chapter 15 for information on adding an external hard drive to your computer.

» An additional or replacement **pointing device** (your mouse is a pointing device), including a trackball or a pen with a tablet, may be more comfortable to use than what came with your computer. Switching between pointing devices helps you avoid repetitive stress. A wireless mouse eliminates the hassle of dealing with a cord. Some people like to add a mouse as an alternative to their laptop's built-in touchpad.

» A **microphone** is crucial for communicating by voice with your computer, through speech recognition, or with your friends over the Internet. A combination headset with microphone may produce the clearest sound.

» A **video camera** (or *webcam*) is essential for video phone calls *à la* the Jetsons. See Chapter 10 for information on using a video camera.

Some of these devices are built into computers; some are not. Most devices that aren't built in connect to a computer using *USB* (Universal Serial Bus) technology. When you connect a device to your computer using a USB cable to the USB port (see **Figure 13-1**), the device identifies itself to the computer. This identification process is called *plug and play.* Ideally, you connect your device, and it simply works.

USB port   **USB cable**

FIGURE 13-1

Windows 10 uses a *device driver* to communicate with an add-on device. The driver is really a program that tells Windows 10 how to run the device. When you connect a device, such as a printer, Windows 10 looks for a driver (in this case, a *printer driver*). That driver may be built into Windows 10, come on a disc that's packaged with the device, or need to be downloaded from the Internet, either automatically by Windows 10 or manually by you.

TIP

Every computer has at least a couple of USB ports. Some are in the front; others are in the back or top of the computer and are harder to reach. If your computer doesn't have enough ports, you can add more by buying a USB hub, which is a small box with two to four USB ports. If a port is hard to reach with a device's cable, you can buy a USB extension cable. Office supply stores may have hubs and cables.

Bluetooth is a wireless technology for adding devices to your computer. If your computer has Bluetooth, you can use Bluetooth as well as USB to add some devices, especially a microphone or headset.

See All Devices

1. Choose Settings on the Start menu. The Settings window opens. Choose Devices to open the Bluetooth & Other Devices category of the Devices window, as shown in **Figure 13-2, top.** Devices listed may include your monitor, speakers, headphones, keyboard, mouse, and more. Devices shared through your network (if your computer is connected to a network) also appear here. For information on adjusting device settings, see the "Access Device Options on the Desktop" section, later in the chapter.

2. Select the Printers & Scanners category in the Devices window, as shown in **Figure 13-2, bottom.** This screen lists printers and scanners that are connected to your computer.

Some, but not all, devices display information below the device name. A network device may display *Offline* (not accessible) or it may display nothing if it is accessible. A printer may display *Ready* or it may display nothing if the printer isn't ready.

You are unlikely to need the Add a Bluetooth or Other Device button because most devices are added *automagically* (that's a word nerds like to use). However, if you select Add a Device, Windows 10 scans for additional hardware. No harm in doing so.

Figure (screenshots)

Settings — Bluetooth & other devices

← Settings — □ ×

⌂ Home

Find a setting

Devices

📶 Bluetooth & other devices
🖨 Printers & scanners
🖱 Mouse
⌨ Typing
🖊 Pen & Windows Ink
▶ AutoPlay
🖧 USB

Bluetooth & other devices

➕ Add Bluetooth or other device

Bluetooth
◯ Off

Mouse, keyboard, & pen

⌨ Lenovo Calliope USB Keyboard

🖱 lenovo USB Optical Mouse

Turn on Bluetooth even faster
To turn Bluetooth on or off without opening Settings, open action center and select the Bluetooth icon.

Related settings
Devices and printers

Sound settings

Display settings

More Bluetooth options

Settings — Printers & scanners

← Settings — □ ×

⌂ Home

Find a setting

Devices

📶 Bluetooth & other devices
🖨 Printers & scanners
🖱 Mouse
⌨ Typing
🖊 Pen & Windows Ink
▶ AutoPlay
🖧 USB

Printers & scanners

Add printers & scanners

➕ Add a printer or scanner

Printers & scanners

🖨 Canon Inkjet MX700 series
Offline

🖨 Fax

🖨 Microsoft Print to PDF

🖨 Microsoft XPS Document Writer

🖨 OneNote

🖨 Send To OneNote 2016

☑ Let Windows manage my default printer

Troubleshoot your printer
If you can't get your printer to work, try running the printer troubleshooter.
Open troubleshooter settings

Related settings
Print server properties

Run the troubleshooter

Help from the web
Downloading print drivers
Scanning documents
Changing printer status

💬 Get help
✒ Give feedback

FIGURE 13-2

Connect a Printer or Other Device

1. Take your printer out of the box. Keep all the packing material together until you know you won't need to return the printer. Arrange all the components for easy access. In addition to the printer, you'll probably find ink cartridges or a toner cartridge, a power cable, and a CD with printer software. Read the setup instructions that come with your printer.

TIP

Some of these steps apply to other devices, such as a mouse, a webcam, or a microphone. Printers often have more packaging and require more assembly than other devices.

2. Remove all tape from the printer. Most printers ship with the print mechanism locked in place to prevent it from moving during shipping. Look for brightly colored tape, paper, or plastic indicating what you need to move or remove to release the print mechanism.

3. Put the printer within cable length of your computer. Insert the ink or toner cartridge before you turn on the printer for the first time. Place some paper in the paper drawer or tray. Connect the printer to the power supply. Plug the printer cable into the printer and into the computer.

TIP

Very likely, you have to download and install a software program from your printer's manufacturer in order to install your printer. Chapter 12 describes how to install programs from a company website.

4. Turn on the printer. A notification tells you that Windows is "setting up a device." If all goes well, you soon see this notification: *Device is ready,* your printer (the brand and model number of your printer) *is set up and ready to go.* You may see other informational messages as Windows 10 handles the configuration.

5. To confirm that your printer is installed properly, see the preceding section, "See All Devices."

Access Device Options on the Desktop

1. For more control over device setup, open the Control Panel to the Devices and Printers window. Press ⊞+D to go to the desktop and then type **control panel** in the Search box on the taskbar. Select Control Panel in the search results to open the Control Panel, and select View Devices and Printers (under Hardware and Sound) to display the window shown in **Figure 13-3**.

2. The Device and Printers window shows the devices attached to your computer, including the computer itself, the display (or monitor), external add-on devices (such as a hard drive, flash drive, or memory card), and the mouse.

TIP

Most of these devices also appear in the Devices category of the Settings app (refer to **Figure 13-2**). However, you'll find options under Devices and Printers that aren't available in the Settings app.

FIGURE 13-3

TIP

Windows 10 automatically installs the Microsoft XPS Document Writer. This device doesn't print but does create files that you can print later using a real printer. For example, if you're in a coffee shop and want to print a web page or an email message, you can use this device and then open the file it creates when your computer is connected to a printer. (That file will open in Acrobat Reader.)

3. Double-click or double-tap the device you want to examine. This action opens the device's properties in a window with options or in a smaller box with limited information and options. (Older devices have more limited information.) **Figure 13-4** shows information about a printer. When you're finished reviewing the information or selecting available options, return to the previous screen using one of these methods:

- If a small box is open, close it.

- If a full-screen dialog box is open, select the back arrow or select Devices and Printers near the top of the window.

4. Display the context menu of options for your printer (or any device) using one of these methods: Click the right mouse button, or tap and hold until you see a small box appear under your finger and then release. Select Printer Properties from the context menu. (Oddly, the menu also has a separate Properties option — be sure to select Printer Properties instead.)

FIGURE 13-4

5. In the Properties window, select the Print Test Page button. Another window opens indicating *A test page has been sent to your printer.* Select Close.

TIP

If a test page doesn't print, check that both ends of the cable are plugged in properly and make sure the printer is turned on. Try to print a test page again. For more help, contact the printer manufacturer or the store where you bought the printer, or search the web.

TIP

If you're having problems with any device, select the Troubleshoot option on the context menu to open a guided troubleshooting program that will walk you through options for resolving problems with the device.

TIP

The top of the Devices and Printers window has the Add a Device and Add a Printer buttons, but you need to use them only if Windows 10 doesn't automatically detect and install your device. With USB and plug-and-play, most devices install automatically.

Calibrate Your Touchscreen

1. If you have a problem accurately selecting objects on your screen using touch, you can calibrate your screen alignment. In this case, calibrating means to help Windows 10 understand what constitutes a tap on the screen. Press ⊞+D to go to the desktop, type **control panel** in the Search box on the taskbar, and select Control Panel in the search results. Then select Hardware and Sound in the Control Panel window. You see the Hardware and Sound window, shown in **Figure 13-5, top.**

2. In the Hardware and Sound window, select Calibrate the Screen for Pen or Touch Input, as shown in **Figure 13-5.** The Tablet PC dialog box appears (refer to **Figure 13-5, bottom**).

Select to calibrate your touchscreen

FIGURE 13-5

3. Select the Calibrate button. User Account Control may ask you to confirm that you want to run the Digitizer Calibration Tool. If so, select Yes.

TIP

If your touchscreen is badly calibrated, you may not be able to tap the Calibrate button. In that case, plug in a mouse to make the selection, and then continue using touch.

4. The screen displays lines around its perimeter, forming a box near the edge of the screen and a second box inside the first about half an inch from the edge. Lines connect these boxes near each corner. The result is 16 intersections. Starting at the upper-left corner, use your finger or a stylus to tap each intersection, which displays two short black lines forming crosshairs. As you touch each intersection, Windows 10 measures your touch and adjusts touch settings accordingly. After each touch is recorded, the crosshairs move to the next intersection to the right. (If the crosshairs don't move, tap the previous intersection again.) As the crosshairs move, tap the highlighted intersection, left to right, down, and then left to right again. The process takes much longer to read about than to do.

TIP

If Windows 10 doesn't recognize your touch, it won't continue with the process. The screen says *Right-click anywhere to return to the last calibration point*. What if you don't have a mouse? Tap and hold until you see the little box under your fingertip, and then release — that's the touch equivalent of a click of the right mouse button.

5. After you have selected each of the 16 calibration points in turn, a box pops up asking whether you want to save the calibration data. Select OK unless you think something went wrong. In that case, select Cancel.

TIP

It's unlikely but possible that you can't continue to the end of the process. If so, the screen says *Press the Esc button to close the tool*. What if you don't have a keyboard? In that case, press and hold the Windows button (the one with the four-part Windows logo) on the tablet edge as you also press the power button, and then release both. On the next screen, select Task Manager. In the Task Manager window, select Digitizer Calibration Tool, and then select the End Task button. (Makes one yearn for an Esc key.)

Chapter **14**

Working with Files

All the data inside your computer is stored on a disk. Your computer has a primary disk, formally called the internal *hard drive*. You may see this disk referred to as the C: drive. (The terms *drive* and *disk* are interchangeable.)

The contents of a disk are organized into individual files. When you create a file and save it for the first time, you create a file on a disk. Many other files on the disk belong to the programs you use, including the thousands of files that make up Windows 10.

Disks also are organized into *folders*, which are containers for files. For its own files, Windows 10 has a main folder that contains dozens of other folders (called *subfolders*). Inside or below that user account folder, Windows 10 creates more folders to help you organize your files by type. For example, by default all your photos go into the Pictures folder, and all your documents go into the Documents folder.

In this chapter, you discover how to save and open a file, search for files, and explore your disk, folders, and files. You work with File Explorer as you create new folders to organize documents and move files from one folder to another. You also copy files from your hard drive to other disks to take with you or give to other people. This chapter also explains how to rename and delete files and folders. What if you delete a file or folder and you regret doing so? Don't worry, because this chapter shows how to get back a file or folder that you mistakenly deleted.

Save and Open a File

1. In computer land, nothing is more important than files. Computer programs are stored in files. Data is stored in files. To start working, you open a file. When you're finished working, you save and close your file. To experiment with files, open WordPad, the word processing app that comes with Windows 10.

TIP

Chapter 2 explains how to open apps. Chapter 8 looks into WordPad and how it can serve your word processing needs.

2. As shown in **Figure 14-1, top,** type a few words into WordPad and then save your file. Most apps (WordPad included) offer three ways to save a file:

- Select the Save button.

- Press Ctrl+S.

- Open the File menu and choose Save.

3. When you save a file for the first time, the Save As dialog box appears (refer to **Figure 14-1, bottom**). It invites you to give the file a name and to tell Windows 10 which folder to keep it in. Enter the name **My File** in the File Name text box. The Save As dialog box offers the means of choosing a folder for your file. For now, you can store your file in the Documents folder, the folder that Windows 10 selected for you (refer to **Figure 14-1, bottom**). Notice that the Documents folder is already selected in the navigation pane on the left side of the Save As dialog box.

4. Select the Save button in the Save As dialog box. Congratulations! You just saved your file. The title bar at the top of the WordPad window shows the name of your file, "My File." When you're not sure what a file is called, look at the title bar along the top of the screen.

5. Close WordPad. The fastest way to close an app is to select the Close button (the X) in the upper-right corner of the screen.

Save button

Let's save this file.

Documents folder   **Enter a name**   **Select Save**

FIGURE 14-1

6. Open WordPad as you did in Step 1. Where is My File, the file you saved and named in Steps 4 and 5?

7. Open the File menu (select the word *File* in the upper-left corner of the screen) and choose Open. The Open dialog box appears, as shown in **Figure 14-2.** This dialog box is the mirror image of the Save As dialog box that you saw earlier. Use it to locate the file you want to open. In this case, Windows 10 has opened the dialog box to its favorite folder, Documents, which also happens to be the folder where My File is stored.

8. Choose My File and then select the Open button (refer to **Figure 14-2**). My File opens onscreen.

Select a folder   **Select a file**   **Select Open**

FIGURE 14-2

TIP

Most apps offer shortcuts for opening files. In WordPad, for example, you see a list of files you recently opened on the File menu. You can select a filename on the list to open a file straightaway.

TIP

To quickly open a file (or application) you opened recently, click or tap in the Search box on the left side of the taskbar. A pop-up menu appears with the names of files you opened recently. You can select a filename in the list to open a file. Select an application name to open an application.

Find a Misplaced File

1. To search for a misplaced file, begin in the Search box. This box is located on the left side of the taskbar. Type the name of a document or photo you have on your computer. The search results panel appears, as shown in **Figure 14-3**.

Narrow the search

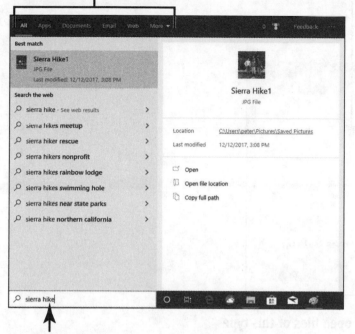

Enter a search term
FIGURE 14-3

TIP

Initially, the search panel shows all and sundry — settings, apps, files, websites, and other search opportunities — in the search results. If you don't see the item you want in a search, narrow the list of items by selecting one of the tabs at the top of the search panel — Apps, Documents, Email, Web, or More. Documents, for example, narrows the search to items on your computer.

2. To open a file, select it in the search results. If more than one application on your computer is capable of opening the file, you may see the How Do You Want to Open This File? dialog box, as shown in **Figure 14-4.** Select an application to open the file.

TIP

The How Do You Want to Open This File? dialog box offers a means of telling Windows 10 to always open files of a certain type with a particular application (refer to **Figure 14-4**). Selecting the Always Use This App to Open check box tells Windows 10 to open files of a certain type automatically with the app you chose.

Choose an application

How do you want to open this file?

Keep using this app

Photos
Photos are easily enhanced, organized for you, and
ready to edit and share.

Other options

Paint

Paint 3D

SketchBook

Snip & Sketch

Look for an app in the Microsoft Store

☐ Always use this app to open .png files

OK

**Select to always open files of this type
with the application you chose**

FIGURE 14-4

3. Close the app that opens the file by using one of these methods:

- Click or tap the Close button (the X located in the upper-right corner of the screen).

- Press Alt+F4.

TIP

Strictly speaking, if you find what you're looking for, stop looking. (No extra charge for pearls of wisdom.) In this case, however, keep looking because doing so reveals important information about how files are organized and how you can take control of that organization.

4. On the desktop, select the File Explorer icon (the yellow folder) in the taskbar. File Explorer opens. Note the *Ribbon,* which is the collapsible toolbar at the top of the window, as shown in **Figure 14-5.**

FIGURE 14-5

TIP

On the Ribbon, tools are grouped by tabs, which in File Explorer consist of File, Home, Share, and View, as well as other tabs that appear based on the selection. Tabs are further divided into sections, labeled below the related tools. (Note, for example, the Clipboard section on the Home tab.) To expand the Ribbon, select the up arrow at the far right of the tabs. Collapse the Ribbon by selecting the down arrow. Select a tab to display its tools, regardless of whether the Ribbon is expanded or collapsed.

5. Select This PC on the left side of the File Explorer window, and then select the box labeled *Search* (probably followed by *This PC*), below the Ribbon and to the right. Type the same search term you used in Step 1. As you type, File Explorer displays any matching files, highlighting the text that matches. **Figure 14-6** shows the results of a search on my computer using the search term *sierra*.

TIP

On a touchscreen, the virtual keyboard doesn't appear on the desktop until you select the keyboard icon on the right side of the taskbar.

FIGURE 14-6

TIP

If the search results include too many files, making it hard to see the one you want, type more of the filename in the Search box. The number of matching files should decrease as you type more text in the box.

6. The *focus* of a search — where File Explorer searches — determines what files and folders are found. In Step 5, you selected This PC, making all the files on your computer the focus of the search. Accordingly, Windows 10 searched for files and folders throughout your computer. To change the focus of your search to the Pictures folder, select the Pictures folder in the navigation pane. Then select the box labeled Search and enter your search term again. The search results focus on files in the Pictures folder.

TIP

You can use Search Tools in the Ribbon to refine a search, as needed. Start a search and then select the Search tab. In the section labeled Refine, select Date Modified and then select a time period ranging from Today to Last Year. Select Kind to limit the search to specific types of files. You can even select by size and other properties.

Add a Location to Quick Access

1. If you frequently access a specific location using File Explorer, you might want to add that location to the Quick Access section of the navigation pane for easy access. The Quick Access section is located at the top of the navigation pane. Windows 10 places some folders in the Quick Access folder list automatically, including the Documents folder and the Pictures folder. As well, it lists in alphabetical order folders that you visit frequently.

2. Display the Quick Access folders. To do so, click or tap the right-pointing arrow next to Quick Access in the navigation pane, as shown in **Figure 14-7.**

Display Quick Access folders

Select a folder and select Pin to Quick Access

FIGURE 14-7

3. Select a folder that you access frequently. For example, if you're currently working on files you keep in a folder called My Work, select that folder in the navigation pane.

4. On the Home tab, select the Pin to Quick Access button (refer to **Figure 14-7**). The name of the folder you selected in Step 3 now appears in the Quick Access folder list. Notice the pin beside its name.

5. Select your folder in the Quick Access folder list. Next time you want to get to this folder, you can get there quickly by selecting Quick Access in the navigation pane and then selecting your folder.

To remove a folder from the Quick Access list, select the folder you want to remove. Then right-click the folder and choose Unpin from Quick Access on the shortcut list.

TIP

Use File Explorer for Easy Access to Files

1. On the desktop, select the File Explorer icon in the taskbar if File Explorer is not already open. The right side of Explorer is called the *content area.* The left side of Explorer is called the *navigation pane* and contains folders. Explorer starts with its focus on your Quick Access and This PC folders, and on your C drive and Network drives (if your computer is connected to a network).

The keyboard shortcut to open File Explorer is ⊞+E.

TIP

2. On the left, select Music, then Pictures, and then Videos, while noting the files in the content area on the right. Many Windows 10 apps store files by default in the Documents, Music, Pictures, and Videos folders. Select the Documents folder again.

3. To create a practice document that you can use in later sections, select the Home tab in the Ribbon. In the New section, select New Item and then select Text Document, as shown in **Figure 14-8.** (If you don't see this option, make sure that the Documents folder is selected.) An empty text document is created and the words *New Text Document* are highlighted so that you can type a new name. Type **practice file.** (You'll rename this file in a later section.) Feel free to repeat this step to create additional items for practice, such as Microsoft Word Documents or Bitmap Images.

Select New Item to create an empty document

FIGURE 14-8

TIP

On a touchscreen, the virtual keyboard doesn't appear on the desktop until you select the keyboard icon on the right side of the taskbar.

4. Select the View tab in the Ribbon. In the Layout section, select each option, such as Extra Large Icons and Large, Medium, and Small Icons. If you see a downward-pointing triangle on the right edge of the Layout options, select that triangle to display even more options. Try them all, if you like.

TIP

Certain layouts are better for certain purposes. For example, photos are easier to recognize as Extra Large Icons than as a List. **Figure 14-9** shows my documents using the Details view, which includes the date the file was modified.

TIP

The more time you spend in File Explorer, the more worthwhile it is to explore the Ribbon as you need it.

Details view shows the modification date

FIGURE 14-9

Create a Folder to Organize Your Files

1. In the File Explorer navigation pane, select the Documents folder.

2. On the Home tab, select the New Folder button. An icon for the new folder appears in the content area on the right, with the name *New folder* next to it and already selected (see **Figure 14-10**).

TIP On a touchscreen, the virtual keyboard doesn't appear on the desktop until you select the keyboard icon on the right side of the taskbar.

3. Type **practice folder** as the new name. Don't move the cursor or mouse before you start typing. Your new text will replace the high-lighted text automatically. Press the Enter key to make the new name stick. (If you have a problem naming the folder, see the "Rename a File or a Folder" section, later in this chapter.)

4. Open your new folder by double-clicking or double-tapping its icon. Notice that the content area is empty.

5. To return to the Documents folder, select Documents in the navigation pane.

FIGURE 14-10

TIP

Don't worry too much about creating folders, because the folders that Windows 10 provides may be all you ever need. As you accumulate more files, however, placing them into other folders can help you stay organized. In the Documents folder, for example, you might create a subfolder called Finances for files related to income, expenses, and investments, and another subfolder called Family for family-related documents. Which folders and subfolders to create and how to name them depends entirely on your own sense of order.

Use Check Boxes to Select Files

1. In File Explorer, you select files to move, copy, rename, or delete. You can add a check box to make selecting multiple files easier. In Explorer, select the View tab and then select the Options button. The Folder Options window appears. Select the View tab (in the Folder Options window, not in the Explorer Ribbon), as shown in **Figure 14-11.** Scroll through the Advanced Settings box until you see Use Check Boxes to Select Items, and then select that check box. Select the OK button.

Select this option

FIGURE 14-11

2. Select the Documents folder (or any folder that contains more than one file). To select a file, click or tap its filename. (You won't see the check box until you select it with a tap or a click, or hover over it with the mouse pointer.) Repeat to select additional files. If you want to deselect a file, select the check box again to remove the check mark. Close the window after you've seen how these check boxes work. **Figure 14-12** shows four selected files.

TIP

If you want to select only a single file, you can select anywhere on the filename. You use the check box when you want to select more than one file at a time.

The Home tab offers other methods for selecting. Select All does just what it says — selects all objects in a folder or library. Select None works similarly. Invert Selection switches the selection. For example, if I chose Invert Selection in the context of **Figure 14-12,** the four selected files would be deselected and all the other files would be selected. Sometimes it's easier to select the files you don't want and then invert the selection.

Select a file by using its check box

Figure showing File Explorer Documents window with item check boxes enabled.

FIGURE 14-12

Add the Undo Button to File Explorer

1. You can add a button to File Explorer to undo an action, such as moving, renaming, or deleting a file. Above the Home tab, select the rather small down-pointing arrow to display the Customize Quick Access Toolbar list, as shown in **Figure 14-13.**

2. Select the Undo option from the drop-down list. The Undo button, which sports a blue arrow curving to the left, appears immediately to the left of the arrow you clicked in Step 1. You can undo most — but not all — actions in File Explorer by clicking or tapping this button immediately after the action. (Time isn't an issue. You can do something and then undo it a year later if you don't do anything in the meantime.)

TIP

The keyboard shortcut for undo is Ctrl+Z. This shortcut works regardless of whether the Undo button is on the screen.

Sometimes, you can undo a series of actions by repeating the undo function.

Customize Quick Access Toolbar menu

FIGURE 14-13

3. Select the Customize Quick Access Toolbar button again. Note that you can also add the Redo button, which, as you would expect, undoes the undo. All the other options appear also on larger buttons on the Home tab, so you don't need to add them to the Quick Access toolbar.

Move a File from One Folder to Another

1. You can move files to organize them. For this exercise, select the Documents folder in File Explorer. Select one of your documents.

TIP

To move more than one file at a time, see the section "Use Check Boxes to Select Files."

On the Home tab, select the Move To button, as shown in **Figure 14-14**.

2. If you see the location you want in the drop-down list, you can select that location. However, for practice, select Choose Location. A window opens, showing every possible location, as shown in **Figure 14-15.** Select Documents and then select the practice folder I tell you how to create in the section "Create a Folder to Organize Your Files," earlier in this chapter. (You can also select the Make New Folder button and name that folder.) Finally, select the Move button.

Select the Move To button

FIGURE 14-14

Unless you move many files or large files, you may not see any indication that the move was completed.

TIP

3. In Explorer, select the folder to which you moved your file. There it is!

Note that the Copy To button in File Explorer works similarly, except that the original file stays where it is and a copy is created in the new location.

TIP

Use these same steps to move a subfolder from one folder to another. However, don't move folders that Windows 10 creates.

TIP

You can move a file in a single step. Click and drag or tap and drag the file to the desired folder. When the file is over the folder, release the mouse button or lift your finger. Although this method can make moving easier, it can also make moving a file to the wrong destination easier. Double-check that the file ends up where you want it before going on to other things.

TIP

Select a location

Move Items ✕

Select the place where you want to move 'Beagle', then click the Move button.

- 📁 Desktop
- > ☁ OneDrive
- > 👤 Peter Weverka
- ∨ 💻 This PC
  - > 🗄 3D Objects
  - > 📁 Desktop
  - ∨ 📄 Documents
    - 📁 Audacity
    - 📁 Custom Office Templates
    - > 📁 Fax
    - 📁 FeedbackHub
    - 📁 My Data Sources
    - 📁 OneNote Notebooks
    - 📁 Outlook Files
    - 📁 Practice Folder
    - > 📁 Scanned Documents
    - 📁 Sound recordings
  - > ⬇ Downloads

Folder: Practice Folder

Make New Folder   Move   Cancel

FIGURE 14-15

Rename a File or a Folder

1. You can change the name of any file or folder you create. (Don't rename files in the Windows or Program Files folders.) For this exercise, select the Documents folder in File Explorer. Then select one of your files.

To rename more than one file at a time, see the section "Use Check Boxes to Select Files," earlier in this chapter. On completion of the rename operation, the files you selected will share the name you provide; each file will have a unique number added to the name, starting with *(1)*.

TIP

2. On the Home tab, select the Rename button. In the content area, the current name of the file or folder is selected, as shown in **Figure 14-16.** If you type anything while the text is selected, you erase the current name, which is convenient if the new name is completely different from the old name. If you want to keep most of the current name and edit it, select inside the name or press the left- or right-arrow key to move to the place in the name where you want to type new text.

3. Type the new name, which can be more than 200 characters long (although a dozen characters may be more than enough). You can capitalize letters and use spaces and dashes, but you can't use slashes or asterisks, which Windows 10 reserves for other purposes.

TIP

On a touchscreen, the virtual keyboard doesn't appear on the desktop until you select the keyboard icon on the right side of the taskbar.

4. When you've typed the new name, press the Enter key to finish the process.

Rename your file

FIGURE 14-16

Delete a File or Folder

1. You can delete any of your files that you no longer need. (Don't delete files in the Windows or Program Files folders.) For this exercise, select the Documents folder in File Explorer. Then select one of your files.

TIP To delete more than one file at a time, see the section "Use Check Boxes to Select Files," earlier in this chapter.

2. On the Home tab, select the X on the Delete button.

TIP The keyboard shortcut to delete the selected file is the Delete key (surprise!).

3. A confirmation dialog box appears and asks whether you really want to delete the file, as shown in **Figure 14-17.** Here's your chance to change your mind, if you want. However, for this exercise, select Yes in the dialog box to delete the file.

TIP If you don't see a confirmation dialog box like the one in **Figure 14-17,** tell Windows 10 that you want to see this dialog box when you delete files and folders. Select the bottom third of the Delete button to display the drop-down list and then select Show Recycle Confirmation.

4. Select another file, and then select the X on the Delete button. The Delete File confirmation window appears. This time, select No to cancel the operation.

TIP You can permanently delete a file, in which case it will not be sent to the Recycle Bin. Select the file, select the bottom of the Delete button, and then select the Permanently Delete option.

FIGURE 14-17

Get Back a File or Folder You Deleted

1. Normally, when you delete a file or folder, Windows 10 moves the object to the Recycle Bin. Objects remain in the Recycle Bin indefinitely, allowing you to restore something you deleted long after you did so. To open the Recycle Bin, go to the desktop and double-click or double-tap the Recycle Bin icon. The Recycle Bin opens, as shown in **Figure 14-18.**

FIGURE 14-18

2. If many files or folders are listed in the Recycle Bin window, type the name of the item you want in the Search box in the top-right corner of the window. If any files match what you type, they appear in the content area.

   Note that on a touchscreen, the virtual keyboard doesn't appear on the desktop until you select the keyboard icon on the right side of the taskbar.

3. To restore a file or folder to its original location, select the file or folder in the Recycle Bin window. On the Manage tab, select Restore the Selected Items. The selected file or folder returns to the folder it was in before it was deleted.

TIP

If Windows 10 needs disk space, it will automatically clear out the oldest files in the Recycle Bin first. If you want to get rid of everything in the Recycle Bin, select the Manage tab and then select Empty Recycle Bin. After you empty the Recycle Bin, you can't undo your action.

TIP

Don't select the Restore All Items button, because doing so puts every single item in the Recycle Bin back in its original location. Most of the files in the Recycle Bin are probably files that you really meant to delete. Choosing this command would be like dumping the trash can on your living-room floor to find a penny you threw away.

See Chapter 15 for information on backing up and restoring files.

Chapter **15**

Backing Up and Restoring Files

S ome of your files — photos and documents — are priceless. If you accidentally delete a treasured file, what can you do but cry? You can insure your well-being by creating copies of your documents and photos.

The best insurance involves storing copies of files on devices separate from your computer. Such devices include the following:

» **Flash drive and memory card:** Carry your files when you're away from your computer by storing them on a portable storage device. For example, you can store files on a USB *flash drive* (also called a *thumb drive*), which is about the size of a disposable cigarette lighter, or a *memory card,* which is the size of a postage stamp and is most often used in laptop computers and digital cameras. Common capacities for flash drives and memory cards range from 2 to 128GB.

TIP
A *gigabyte* (GB) of storage can hold thousands of files, but you'll be amazed by how quickly you can fill that space.

» **External hard drive:** This type of drive has a much higher capacity than a flash drive, making it ideal for backing up all your files — the best insurance. Affordable external hard drives range from 500GB to 3TB.

TIP

A *terabyte* (TB) of storage is equal to a thousand gigabytes, which should be enough room to back up everything on your computer.

» **Network drive:** If your computer connects to a home network, you may be able to copy files to other devices on the network. For example, you can use a large-capacity network drive to back up files from more than one computer.

» **OneDrive:** Your Microsoft Account comes with 5 gigabytes of free storage in the cloud (on the Internet). Anything stored in OneDrive is duplicated on additional computers you log in to with the same Microsoft Account.

TIP

OneDrive provides storage but not a backup (duplicate). If you delete a file from OneDrive, any copies stored on linked computers are also deleted.

In this chapter, you copy files to a flash drive and hard drive so that you can transport files between machines and back up your files. You also find out how to store files in the Microsoft cloud with OneDrive. As well, you use the Backup function, which automatically copies files as a backup. Consider this scenario: You write a letter to a friend and save it to your Documents folder. Later that day, you delete part of the letter and save it again, replacing the original document. The next day, you wish you still had the deleted text. The Backup function comes to your rescue because it saves versions of files; you can recover the latest version or an earlier version of a file. As I wrote this book, I saved it hundreds of times — the Backup function could save every version, allowing me to roll back to an earlier copy, to before I had made some big goof. (That's purely hypothetical, of course.)

Finally, in this chapter, you explore the Reset function, a tool you may need if you have problems with your computer. The Reset function reinstalls Windows 10 but preserves your personal data.

Add an External Hard Drive or Flash Drive

1. Before you attach a flash drive or hard drive to your computer, consider the following options that Windows 10 automatically offers for using the newly attached drive:

   - **Configure Storage Settings** opens the Settings app so that you can configure the storage settings on your computer.

   - **Open Folder to View Files** displays the contents of the disk in File Explorer on the desktop. You select this option to copy files to or from the drive you're attaching.

   - **Take No Action** dismisses the notification.

   TIP Notifications appear for the amount of time specified in PC Settings. If the notification disappears before you can select it, you can redisplay it by removing and then reinserting the drive or USB cable.

2. Locate an unused USB port on your computer. A *USB port* is a small rectangular slot on the front or back of a desktop computer or along any edge of a laptop or tablet computer. USB ports are often marked with a symbol that looks like a trident, as shown in **Figure 15-1.**

USB symbol

USB flash drive   **USB port**

FIGURE 15-1

TIP

If a USB port is hard to reach, you can buy an extension cable from any office supply store. You can also buy a *hub*, which adds ports to your computer.

3. If you're using a flash drive, insert it into the USB slot. USB fits one way only. If you're using an external hard drive, plug it into a power source, if one is required, and then connect a cable to the USB port. Turn on the external drive, if it has a separate power switch. (Flash drives and some external hard drives don't have separate power supplies or switches.)

4. Windows 10 displays a notification to *Choose what to do with removable drives*. (You can click the mouse instead of tapping.) If you select the first notification, a list of choices appears, as shown in **Figure 15-2.** If you know which action you want to take, you can select that action. Otherwise, select Take No Action or wait until the notification disappears on its own.

USB Drive (E:)

Choose what to do with removable drives.

Configure storage settings
Settings

Open folder to view files
File Explorer

Take no action

FIGURE 15-2

Copy Files to or from a Flash Drive

1. To copy files or folders to a flash drive, insert the flash drive into one of your computer's USB ports.

TIP

Laptops, like cameras, often have a slot for a memory card. Want to turn your memory card into a flash drive? Simply buy a device called a dedicated or single-purpose memory card reader. Strictly speaking, a multipurpose card reader also works, but multicard readers cost more and are often larger than single-card readers. In addition, a dedicated memory card reader doesn't need a cable to connect a camera to a computer. You can just download your pictures to your hard drive from the card.

2. If Windows 10 displays a notification (refer to **Figure 15-2**) when you insert the flash drive or memory card, select Open Folder to View Files, which will open File Explorer on the desktop. If File Explorer doesn't open automatically, go to the desktop and then select the yellow folder icon in the taskbar to open File Explorer.

TIP

The keyboard shortcut to open File Explorer is ▥+E.

3. In File Explorer, navigate on the left to the folder that contains the files you want to copy. See Chapter 14 for information on navigating in File Explorer. Select the folder.

4. On the right side of File Explorer, select the folder or file you want to copy. If you see a check box to the left of each object you want to copy, you can select each check box to copy multiple files simultaneously. (If you don't see check boxes next to files, see Chapter 14 for information on enabling this function for file selection.)

TIP

To select every object on the right simultaneously, use the Select All button on the Home tab. You can also select the files you don't want to copy and then use the Invert Selection button on the Home tab; deselected files become selected and vice versa. You can select files in other ways as well.

The keyboard shortcut to select all files in File Explorer is Ctrl+A.

5. In the Ribbon, select the Home tab and then select the Copy To button, as shown in **Figure 15-3**. Select Choose Location from the menu that appears.

TIP

You can move files if you want them gone from their original location. To do so, select the Move To button. Follow the remaining steps, but substitute the word *Move* for *Copy*.

6. In the Copy Items window, under the This PC heading, locate the flash drive or memory card. The drive will not be Local Disk (C:), where Windows 10 resides. Select the removable flash drive or memory card to which you want to copy the files, as shown in **Figure 15-4,** and then select the Copy button. If the files copy quickly, you may not see any indication of progress; otherwise, a progress bar is displayed until copying is complete.

Select the Copy To button

FIGURE 15-3

Select a location for the copy

FIGURE 15-4

TIP

OneDrive may be listed in the Copy Items window. Files you copy to OneDrive are automatically copied to the cloud and to linked computers.

7. If you copy a file that is already on the destination disk, the Replace or Skip Files window appears, as shown in **Figure 15-5.** (Perhaps you're copying a newer version of a file you copied before.) Note the available options:

   - **Replace the File in the Destination:** Selecting this option replaces one file with another. Be certain that you don't need the replaced file (as you might if you want to keep different versions of files).

   - **Skip This File:** Selecting this option does nothing with this file.

   - **Compare Info for Both Files:** Selecting this option opens another window in which you can select files on the left to replace those on the right, and select files on the right to keep. Selecting the same file on the left and right creates a second file with a number added to the name, such as *my file (2)*. This option enables you to have the original and the new file.

   Select one of the previous options. If you selected Compare Info for Both Files, select the files to replace or skip, and then select the Continue button. You may or may not see a progress indicator, depending on how quickly the files are copied.

8. Confirm that the copy worked by navigating on the left to the location you selected as the destination in Step 6. If the files are there, congratulations; you're done. If not, try Steps 4 through 6 again.

9. Remove the flash drive or memory card you inserted in Step 1. You're good to go.

TIP

If you have files or folders that you'd be devastated to lose, follow the steps in this task to create backup copies of those items on a portable storage device. Then keep that device in a safe place.

TIP

To copy files from a flash drive or memory card, follow these same steps but select the flash drive in Step 3 and the folder or other destination to which you want to copy or move files in Step 6.

Replace or Skip Files — □ ✕

Copying 1 item from Saved Pictures to USB Drive (E:)

The destination already has a file named "094.JPG"

✓ Replace the file in the destination

➧ Skip this file

🗗 Compare info for both files

ⓥ More details

FIGURE 15-5

Use OneDrive to Store File Copies

1. Use OneDrive to back up and store files on the Microsoft cloud — in other words, to back up and store files on servers that Microsoft maintains on the Internet. If you have a Microsoft Account, you are entitled to 5 gigabytes of free storage space on the Microsoft cloud. If you have an Office 365 subscription, you are entitled to 1,054 giga-bytes (1 terabyte). Here's the big advantage of OneDrive: You can access files that you keep on the cloud from any computer connected to the Internet, whether you're in Tallahassee or Timbuktu. Use one of these techniques to open the Set Up OneDrive dialog box and tell Windows 10 that you want to use OneDrive:

- Select the OneDrive icon in the notification area located in the lower-right corner of the screen.

- Enter **onedrive** in the Search box and select the OneDrive desk-top app in the pop-up menu.

TIP

If you're signed in with a Microsoft Account, Windows 10 already knows your password. Skip to Step 3.

2. In the Set Up OneDrive dialog box, enter your email address and select the Sign In button. In the dialog box that appears, enter the password to your email account and select the Sign In button.

3. As shown in **Figure 15-6,** the next dialog box welcomes you to OneDrive or tells you where your OneDrive folder is located (which dialog box you see depends on whether you are signed in with a

Microsoft or a local account). Click the Next button or Close button as necessary. You're ready to copy the folders you want to back up or store into your OneDrive folder in the Microsoft cloud.

FIGURE 15-6

4. Open File Explorer and copy the folders you want to back up or store into the OneDrive folder. As shown in **Figure 15-7,** this folder appears in the folder panel on the left side of the File Explorer window. Don't let appearances fool you. Although the OneDrive folder appears alongside the other folders in the folders panel, that folder lives in the Microsoft cloud, not on your computer. Folders and files on OneDrive show a green check mark to let you know they're on OneDrive (refer to **Figure 15-7**).

> Chapter 14 explains how to copy and move files with File Explorer. As well, it explains how to create and save files.

TIP

5. In File Explorer, open one of the folders on your computer that you copied to OneDrive, create a new file, and save the new file under the name **Sync** in the folder you opened.

6. In File Explorer, select the OneDrive folder and then, in OneDrive, open the folder with the same name as the folder you opened in Step 5. You see the Sync file on OneDrive. When you save a file in a folder that is also kept on OneDrive, a copy of the file is made to OneDrive automatically. Microsoft calls this *syncing* (for synchronizing). Thanks to syncing, you don't have to copy files to OneDrive on your own because the copies are made automatically.

OneDrive folder   **Check marks indicate files and folders stored on OneDrive**

FIGURE 15-7

TIP

To see which folders from your computer are synced to folders in OneDrive, select the OneDrive icon in the notification area, choose More on the pop-up menu, and then choose Settings. The Microsoft OneDrive dialog box appears. On the Account tab, select the Choose Folders button. The Choose Folders dialog box appears, as shown in **Figure 15-8.** You can deselect a folder in this dialog box to prevent OneDrive from syncing a folder on your computer to its counterpart folder on OneDrive. Deselect a folder if you don't care to back up its contents on OneDrive.

7. Start the Edge browser and go to the OneDrive online website at this address: onedrive.live.com. If necessary, enter your password. You see the folders from your computer that you store on OneDrive, as shown in **Figure 15-9.** You can manage your files and folders starting here. For example, you can delete, move, and download files and folders.

TIP

Chapter 6 shows how to use Edge, the official web browser of Windows 10.

Choose which folder to sync

FIGURE 15-8

FIGURE 15-9

Turn On File History

1. To enable Windows 10 to create backup copies of your files, first make sure that an external drive such as a hard drive or flash drive is connected to your computer. Then select the Start button and choose Settings on the Start menu.

2. In the Settings window, select Update & Security. Then select Backup in the Update & Security window. The Backup screen opens, as shown in **Figure 15-10, top.** Which screen you see depends on whether you have told Windows 10 where you want to keep backup copies of your files. If your screen looks like **Figure 15-10, bottom,** Windows 10 already recognizes where your backup drive is located; skip to Step 4.

3. Select Add a Drive, and in the Select a Drive window, choose a backup drive on the list (refer to **Figure 15-10**).

TIP

File History stores information on an external drive or a network location. After you turn on File History, it will automatically create copies of your documents and photos on the drive you identify. If you lose, delete, or change your mind about changes to a file, you can restore the backup copy created by File History following the steps in the "Restore Files with File History" section, later in this chapter.

4. Turn on the Automatically Back Up My Files setting (shown in **Figure 15-10, bottom**) if this setting isn't already turned on.

5. Select More Options to tell Windows 10 which folders to back up and how often to back up the folders. The Backup Options screen opens, as shown in **Figure 15-11.** By default, Windows 10 saves copies of files every hour, but you can change this and other file history settings, as follows:

Select Add a Drive to indicate where the backup drive is

Backup

Back up using File History

Back up your files to another drive and restore them if the originals are lost, damaged, or deleted.

＋ Add a drive

More options

Choose the right backup option for you

To have Windows back up your files to a safe place, choose where you want your files to go—to the cloud, an external storage device, or a network.

Learn more about backup options

Backup

Back up using File History

Back up your files to another drive and restore them if the originals are lost, damaged, or deleted.

Automatically back up my files

◯ On

More options

Looking for an older backup?

If you created a backup using the Windows 7 Backup and Restore tool, it'll still work in Windows 10.
Go to Backup and Restore (Windows 7)

Choose the right backup option for you

To have Windows back up your files to a safe place, choose where you want your files to go—to the cloud, an external storage device, or a network.

Learn more about backup options

Help from the web

Mapping a network drive

🛈 Get help
✎ Give feedback

Turn on File History

FIGURE 15-10

- **Back Up My Files:** This option controls how frequently File History checks for new or changed files. I recommend that you select Every 10 Minutes to minimize the chances of losing new or changed documents.

TIP

When you go on vacation, consider disconnecting the external drive and storing it in a fireproof safe or a safe deposit box. The drive is your insurance against theft or destruction.

- **Keep My Backups:** By default, File History keeps copies of your files forever. This option allows you to limit how long copies are kept. Leave this set as Forever.

FIGURE 15-11

- **Back Up These Folders:** File History provides a laundry list of folders to back up.

  To remove a folder, select it in the list. The Remove button appears. Select this button.

  To add a folder, select the Add a Folder button. Then select the folder in the Select Folder dialog box.

- **Back Up to a Different Drive:** Select the Stop Using Drive button and repeat Steps 1 through 3 to choose a different external drive for keeping backup copies of your files.

TIP

To turn off automatic backups or start backing up to another drive, return to the Backup window (refer to **Figure 15-10**) and select the More Options link. Then scroll to the bottom of the Backup Options dialog box (refer to **Figure 15-11**) and select the Stop Using Drive button. At that point, if you want to back up to a different drive, start all over (repeat Steps 3 through 5).

Restore Files with File History

1. In the Search box on the taskbar, type **file history.** On the search results screen, select Restore Your Files with File History – Control Panel. File History opens on the desktop.

2. Select the Restore Personal Files link. You see a screen similar to the one in **Figure 15-12.**

FIGURE 15-12

3. The most recent backup versions created by File History appear in the window. To see other versions of backups, select the left-pointing arrow at the bottom of the window. To return to the most recent backup, select the right-pointing arrow.

TIP

Don't select the Restore button until you select the specific file(s) you want. Otherwise, all files will be restored simultaneously.

TIP

Generally, you want to restore the most recent version of a file. However, if you want to restore content that you changed prior to the most recent version, browse to an earlier backup.

4. If you know the location of the file you want to restore, you can open that location with a double-click or double-tap. If you're not sure of the location, select the Search All box in the upper-right corner and type the document name. Matching results appear as you type. Select the file you want to restore.

5. Select the Restore button. If you restored a file you previously deleted, you can close File History. Skip the remaining steps.

6. If the Replace or Skip Files window opens (refer to **Figure 15-5**) in the preceding step, a different version of the file exists in the original location. If you're sure you want to restore the previous version of the file, you can choose Replace the Files in the Destination. However, to see additional options, select Let Me Decide for Each File. The File Conflicts window appears, as shown in **Figure 15-13.**

FIGURE 15-13

7. In the File Conflict window, consider the following selections:

- Select files on the left to replace files in the destination with the backup files. (This is the same as selecting Replace on the Replace or Skip Files screen.)

- Select files on the right to cancel restoring those files. (This is the same as selecting Skip on the Replace or Skip Files screen.)

- If you select the same files on both sides of the window, File History will leave the original as is and restore the backup version with the same name plus *(2)*, allowing you to have both versions. (You need this option only if you're uncertain about which version you want.)

If you're restoring multiple files at the same time, you can select different options for each: replace one, skip another, and have File History create a copy for another. That's a lot of choices in one little window.

8. Select Continue, and Windows 10 completes the operation based on your choices in Step 7. The location of the restored files opens in File Explorer.

Reset a Misbehaving Computer

1. Glitch happens. The computer misbehaves, a program crashes, or the machine becomes unexpectedly slow. If your computer is misbehaving, try resetting it. Click the Start button and choose Settings. In the Settings window, select Update & Security. In the Update & Security window, select Recovery.

Before you reset your PC, see Chapter 12 for information about updating and maintaining Windows 10. Updating Windows may resolve some problems.

The Reset function should leave your data alone and unchanged. However, consider following Steps 1–4 in the section "Restore Files with File History" to confirm that your external drive contains all your files. Better safe than sorry.

2. Under Reset This PC, select the Get Started button, as shown in **Figure 15-14.**

This is where you want to click

Recovery

Reset this PC

If your PC isn't running well, resetting it might help. This lets you choose to keep your personal files or remove them, and then reinstall Windows.

Get started

Go back to the previous version of Windows 10

This option is no longer available because your PC was updated more than 10 days ago.

Get started

Learn more

Advanced startup

Start up from a device or disc (such as a USB drive or DVD), change your PC's firmware settings, change Windows startup settings, or restore Windows from a system image. This will restart your PC.

Restart now

Settings sidebar:
- Home
- Find a setting
- **Update & Security**
- Windows Update
- Delivery Optimization
- Windows Security
- Backup
- Troubleshoot
- Recovery
- Activation
- Find my device
- For developers
- Windows Insider Program

Right sidebar:
Fix problems without resetting your PC

Resetting your PC can take a while. If you haven't already, try running a troubleshooter to resolve issues before you reset.

Troubleshoot

Help from the web

Finding my BitLocker recovery key

Creating a recovery drive

Get help

Give feedback

FIGURE 15-14

TIP

The Reset function doesn't remove apps installed through the Microsoft Store but does remove any apps you installed any other way. This safety feature is based on the assumption that something you installed from some other source is causing a problem. Be certain that you either don't need a desktop app or you have the materials necessary to reinstall a desktop app, such as Microsoft Office. Windows 10 will create a file on the desktop after the fact, identifying the programs it removed.

3. In the Choose an Option dialog box, select Keep My Files. (Or select Cancel, if you're just exploring this feature and don't want to continue with it.)

4. Reset runs, and your computer will restart at least once. When the reset process is complete, the Lock screen appears. Sign in as usual. If you see a file named *Removed Apps* on the desktop, double-click or double-tap it to open that file in your browser. The removed apps are listed. If you're aware that one of these apps created a problem, don't reinstall it.

TIP

Don't be intimidated by the Reset function — it's easy, quick, and worthwhile if it makes a problem computer run better.

Index

O

Office 365, 282

OneDrive
  overview, 276
  storing files on, 282–285

Open Conversation button, 165

Open dialog box, 102

Open Folder to View Files option, 277

opening
  apps, 28–32
  files, 254–256
  multiple desktops, 99–101
  tabs, 114–115

operating system (OS), 9

optical disk drive, 218

organizing
  files, 264–265
  photos, 196–198

OS (operating system), 9

Outlook, 129

P

Page keys, 14

passwords
  case-sensitive, 75
  for local account, 82–85
  security and, 80
  signing in with, 74
  for Wi-Fi connections, 68

pasting, 191

People App, 146–149

peripherals, 243

Personal Email field, 147

Personalization screen, 25

desktop image and, 101–103
  on Windows Settings screen, 25

Photo quality option, 188

photos. *See also* audio; videos
  folders for, 186
  importing, 189–193
  overview, 185
  scanning, 202–204
  taking with camera on computer, 186–187

Photos App
  editing photos with, 199–201
  organizing photos with, 196–198
  printing photos with, 201–202
  viewing photos with, 193–196

pinching, 12

pinning
  folders, 261–262
  icons to Taskbar, 103–104
  in Weather app, 39

pixel, 188

Play and Explore group, 45

playlists
  copying audio with, 218
  creating, 213–216

Play/Pause button, 208

Plug and Play hardware
  installing and, 249
  overview, 244–246

pointer

defined, 11
  links and, 110
  moving with touchpad, 10
  resize pointer, 95
  settings for, 58

pointing device, 244

ports
  for memory card, 278–279
  for USB, 277–278

power button
  on computer, 18
  on flash drive, 278
  pressing Windows button and, 252

pressing keys, 13

Preview box, 60

previous button, 208

printers. *See also* hardware
  benefits of, 244
  connecting to, 247–248
  overview, 243
  printing, 201–202

Private event in Calendar app, 152

programs. *See* apps

progress bar, 279

Q

Quick Access toolbar
  adding location to, 261–262
  overview, 93

Quick Actions panel, 63

Quick Status settings, 162–163

QWERTY keyboards, 14

About the Author

Peter Weverka is the best-selling author of many *For Dummies* books, including *Office 365 All-in-One For Dummies*, as well as four dozen other books about various topics. Peter's humorous articles and stories (not related to computers, thankfully) have appeared in *Harper's*, *SPY*, and other magazines for grown-ups.

Dedication

For Bruce

Author's Acknowledgments

Thanks to Mark Justice Hinton for writing the first edition of this book. Much of Mark's work lives on in this edition. I would also like to thank Ashley Coffey at Wiley for giving me the opportunity to write this book and Susan Christophersen for editing it. Thanks as well go to Ryan Williams, the technical editor, who made sure all instructions were accurate.

Publisher's Acknowledgments

Acquisitions Editor: Ashley Coffey

Project Manager and Copy Editor: Susan Christophersen

Proofreader: Debbye Butler

Technical Editor: Ryan Williams

Production Editor: Mohammed Ali Zafar

Cover Image:
© Sam Edwards/Getty Images

Leverage the power

Dummies is the global leader in the reference category and one of the most trusted and highly regarded brands in the world. No longer just focused on books, customers now have access to the dummies content they need in the format they want. Together we'll craft a solution that engages your customers, stands out from the competition, and helps you meet your goals.

Advertising & Sponsorships

Connect with an engaged audience on a powerful multimedia site, and position your message alongside expert how-to content. Dummies.com is a one-stop shop for free, online information and know-how curated by a team of experts.

- Targeted ads
- Video
- Email Marketing
- Microsites
- Sweepstakes sponsorship

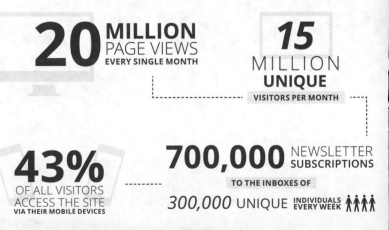

20 MILLION PAGE VIEWS EVERY SINGLE MONTH

15 MILLION UNIQUE VISITORS PER MONTH

43% OF ALL VISITORS ACCESS THE SITE VIA THEIR MOBILE DEVICES

700,000 NEWSLETTER SUBSCRIPTIONS TO THE INBOXES OF *300,000* UNIQUE INDIVIDUALS EVERY WEEK

# of dummies

Custom Publishing

Reach a global audience in any language by creating a solution that will differentiate you from competitors, amplify your message, and encourage customers to make a buying decision.

- Apps
- Books
- eBooks
- Video
- Audio
- Webinars

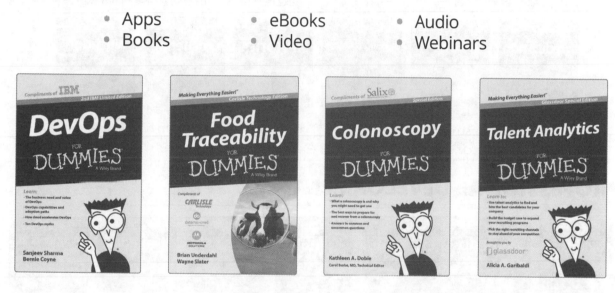

Brand Licensing & Content

Leverage the strength of the world's most popular reference brand to reach new audiences and channels of distribution.

For more information, visit dummies.com/biz

PERSONAL ENRICHMENT

Staying Sharp

9781119187790
USA $26.00
CAN $31.99
UK £19.99

Facebook

9781119179030
USA $21.99
CAN $25.99
UK £16.99

Guitar

9781119293354
USA $24.99
CAN $29.99
UK £17.99

Investing

9781119293347
USA $22.99
CAN $27.99
UK £16.99

Beekeeping

9781119310068
USA $22.99
CAN $27.99
UK £16.99

Digital Photography

9781119235606
USA $24.99
CAN $29.99
UK £17.99

Meditation

9781119251163
USA $24.99
CAN $29.99
UK £17.99

Pregnancy

9781119235491
USA $26.99
CAN $31.99
UK £19.99

Samsung Galaxy S 7

9781119279952
USA $24.99
CAN $29.99
UK £17.99

iPhone

9781119283133
USA $24.99
CAN $29.99
UK £17.99

Crocheting

9781119287117
USA $24.99
CAN $29.99
UK £16.99

Nutrition

9781119130246
USA $22.99
CAN $27.99
UK £16.99

PROFESSIONAL DEVELOPMENT

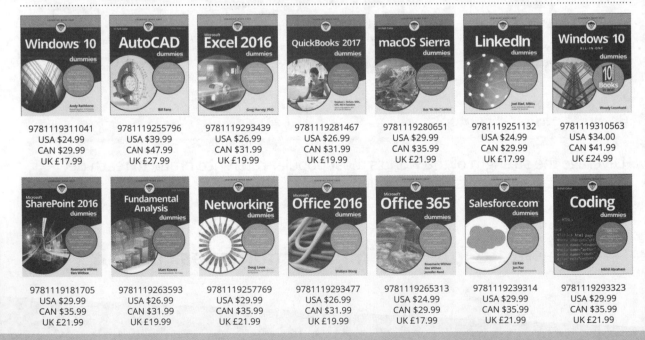

Windows 10

9781119311041
USA $24.99
CAN $29.99
UK £17.99

AutoCAD

9781119255796
USA $39.99
CAN $47.99
UK £27.99

Excel 2016

9781119293439
USA $26.99
CAN $31.99
UK £19.99

QuickBooks 2017

9781119281467
USA $26.99
CAN $31.99
UK £19.99

macOS Sierra

9781119280651
USA $29.99
CAN $35.99
UK £21.99

LinkedIn

9781119251132
USA $24.99
CAN $29.99
UK £17.99

Windows 10

9781119310563
USA $34.00
CAN $41.99
UK £24.99

SharePoint 2016

9781119181705
USA $29.99
CAN $35.99
UK £21.99

Fundamental Analysis

9781119263593
USA $26.99
CAN $31.99
UK £19.99

Networking

9781119257769
USA $29.99
CAN $35.99
UK £21.99

Office 2016

9781119293477
USA $26.99
CAN $31.99
UK £19.99

Office 365

9781119265313
USA $24.99
CAN $29.99
UK £17.99

Salesforce.com

9781119239314
USA $29.99
CAN $35.99
UK £21.99

Coding

9781119293323
USA $29.99
CAN $35.99
UK £21.99

dummies.com